T0171330

Tucson:
With An Olive and Twist

JoAn Stolley

iUniverse, Inc.
New York Bloomington

Tucson: With An Olive and Twist

iUniverse books may be ordered through booksellers or by contacting:

iUniverse
1663 Liberty Drive
Bloomington, IN 47403
www.iuniverse.com
1-800-Authors (1-800-288-4677)

ISBN: 978-1-4401-4242-0 (pbk)
ISBN: 978-1-4401-4241-3 (ebook)

Printed in the United States of America

iUniverse rev. date: 7/07/09

Dedication

This is dedicated to my husband, who shares his gifts of healing and spirituality with me, and to those other people and creatures that have walked beside me at one time or another. You continue to be my inspiration! A bouquet, lingering with the fragrance of exotic flowers, for each of you!

Foreword

Through my journey to arrange and publish this collection of short stories and poetry, I hope I have been successful in distilling words to touch the common experiences that make us all so human.

This is a work of fiction and not intended to represent specific persons.

Contents

Chapter 1: Tucson: With an Olive and Twist

The journey of midlife

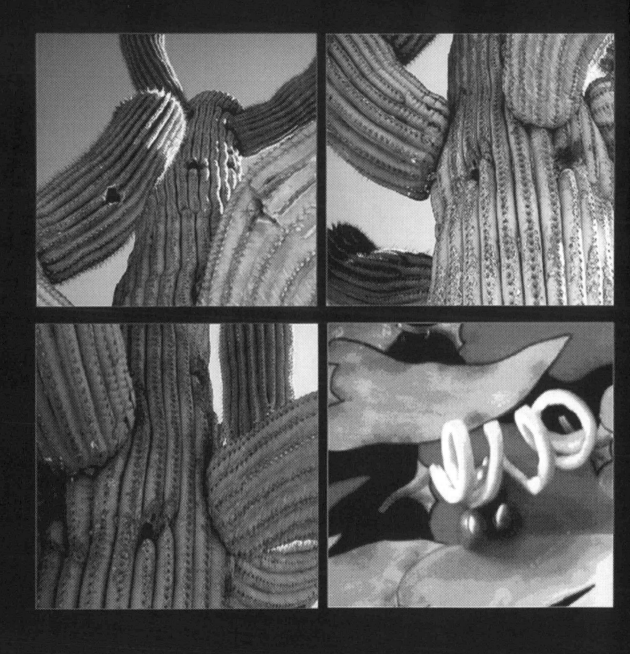

Tucson: With an Olive and Twist

Everyone has a Tucson in their life. My mind has wafted up through two-story windows—something out of a Western-style interior-design magazine—and is caught in the purplish, boiling colors of the July monsoon sky as it moves across the Santa Catalina Mountains. Served with Southwestern panache, a martini lubricates my retrospection. I never imagined I would be *here* in Tucson.

First Time Around

Tucson was a business trip. Stepping out of Tucson International Airport, a duet of saguaro sentinels confronts you as if a rigorous border interrogation is inevitable. These towering Sonoran Desert cacti take me aback. I'm comfortable with my urban lifestyle. I immediately sense it is too stark and barren here for me.

With its constant infusion of mixed ethnicities, Tucson is settled comfortably into the silence of the Sonoran Desert. It's almost like an island culture—only this is an island in the vastness of desert. Playing the role of a Mexican territory, a Spanish military outpost, and a bartering chip in the 1854 Gadsden Purchase are all parts of its past. I always ask people what brings them to Tucson. Their answers are spiced with flavors of personal hardship, wanderlust spirit, family ties, and sun-loving health reasons.

After less than a week in the Tucson Valley, I knew it was a new life destination. Coveys of Gambel's quail scooting along the desert's dusty floor among the thickets of prickly pear sent my heart the message to stay here. With no patience for weakness in any creature, the desert is an absolute, unforgiving environment. Ironically, it is also a habitat rich in ecosystems and teeming with life. I am in my mid fifties, and the sporting, top-knotted quail have beckoned me to come, to transform, and to dance among the Southwestern rhythms—more vibrantly alive than ever before.

The logistical challenges of a cross-country move didn't cause a pause in my thinking about the prospects of relocating. It was one of those intense moments of personal realization. Of course, there are subtle differences between self-realization and impulsiveness. How much of each was at play was something I would have to quietly figure out along the way.

The twist in my life was that I was now Tucson bound. It's the whispering inner voices that persevere in suggesting new and unusual patterns and colors for our lives. Listening to them is risky. They feel like the strike of spectacular, vertical bolts of monsoon lightening from the desert summer rains. When a new pathway comes, it takes courage to make choices. There will always be turning points and new choices, whether we welcome them or not. To a polite inquiry a couple of years ago about my intended life direction, I would have certainly uttered nothing about Tucson. A move is preposterous! Give up the comforts of metropolitan living? That's just madness, for sure.

Interstate Trekking

Spring seemed the appropriate time to drive our first household shipment to Tucson. I had it wired in my head that this would be mostly a physical trip, concentrating solely on packing and an onerous two thousand-mile drive to a new and mostly unfamiliar destination in the Sonoran Desert. The fact that my cherished East Coast home was being torn asunder and this trip was actually underway still hadn't penetrated on any significant emotional level.

Thus began the arduous, cross-country journey in a Sherman-like moving truck with a small, hitched trailer doggedly swaying behind. At some point after crossing the Mississippi, a soulful prayer was mumbled as protection against the possibility of the weighted trailer just evaporating into the sunset. Of course, that didn't happen. Thankfully, the trip to Tucson went safely and without incident.

After a couple hundred miles brushing with the western slopes of Virginia's Appalachian Mountains, the physical journey went into automatic cruise control. However, something quite different was pressing to come along on the accompanying self-journey. Thoughts of such a personal, radical change repeatedly ignited cold sweats. The move was totally out of character for me and certainly outside my comfort zone—in fact, I surmised it was somewhere in the range of the planet Jupiter!

The physical side of the trip was merely a backdrop to what was going on in my sense of self-awakening. Coming to stark realization that thirty years of work and endless commuting would be abruptly wrapped into retirement gave me pause. Anxiety wafted heavily among the smells of the povidone-iodine scrubs that had been prescribed for my impending surgery. The journey to Tucson would certainly change the equilibrium of my marital relationship as well. Pondering this concoction of events was making me light-headed.

Could my trip be compared to one of those exclusive spas retreats where you can totally immerse yourself in self-indulgent behavior to flush your body of toxins and fat? In a peculiar way, it was. A mind-crushing difference was that I was trundling along the highway, doing the toxin release thing cold turkey! I scrunched up close to the truck's side mirror to take a realistic look at my face in the raw sunlight—it was ego wrenching. Red blotches were erupting, uninvited, across my skin. However, the now-remembered blemishes in my career, marriages, and relationships were what mainly reflected back at me through that wretched mirror.

What the interstate miles did is allow me private reflection time as the countryside skimmed by. During the miles to Tucson, I had the moments to explore and purge what was destructive. Like the gathering monsoon skies filled with crackling energy, I had to be bold to strike personal change at this most vulnerable midpoint in my life. I have been too content inhaling the rarified air within my personal bell jar only to discover, in traveling this road, how stagnant parts of my life have really become.

It would certainly have been much, much easier never to go to Tucson.

Merging with Tennessee I-40

Tennessee spring rains shellacked the state's famous limestone into dark, jagged hues, both in the highway median and along its roadsides. The redbuds were in full, deep pink blossom. Traveling along, it seemed as if some super-sized Ikebana arrangement of these redbuds, fanning between the limestone protrusions, would stream along the road forever. I imagine that most travelers along the interstate missed the spectacle of this scenery entirely. Their lives' immediate purpose was to hover just above the speed limit and below state patrollers' radar range, honking in frustration at having to suffer the indignity of passing our little caravan consisting of a truck and trailer. How much do we miss in life by zooming down our personal interstates just for the sake of reaching a destination—and another destination, and yet another?

Road signage told us Knoxville and I-40 were straight ahead. My gut-deep stomach knot was counterbalancing my childlike sense of adventure. Merging onto westbound I-40 was a significant break with all that has been familiar over these many years. It's as if, now, in Tennessee, I can almost pick up the smells of the musky-scented Sonoran Desert rains. For the first time, I feel instinctively that this drive will turn out okay. I had finally come to terms with my Tucson decision.

Towards Fort Smith

The westward route on I-40 across Arkansas was mostly tedious until the vastness of the skies abruptly commandeered my attention. Late afternoon was just starting to usher in a spectacular sunset, with the highway cutting straight towards the horizon. Enormous arcs of bluish and pale orchid colors crisscrossed each other among the pearl-shaded cirrus clouds as the dramatic plays of tangerine and crimson pinks emanated from the disappearing Arkansas sunset.

The tiredness of long miles of driving momentarily evaporated. It was as if there were nothing in the universe except this vehicle, the forever-gray concrete ribbon of highway, and being subsumed upward into the colors of the sky. Feeling such unity of purpose was exhilarating. Everything became one. A floating, physically freeing sensation overpowered my body. Perhaps my tiredness meant I was hallucinating, but my sudden desire to be totally engulfed within the raucous play of sunset colors was very real. It felt impulsive, out-of-control, and wonderful!

With darkness rapidly approaching, we exercised a hunch to stop and rest for the night in Fort Smith. Tonight, the flat-going Oklahoma and Texas Panhandle seemed an interminable I-40 stretch on the printed map.

Oh! Santa Rosa

Stretch goals in life are wonderful. It's those very difficult goals that you set for yourself and then wonder how you will ever attain them. As life gets more complicated, these goals get simpler. Ours was crossing the New Mexico border before sundown, after having left Fort Smith at a very early hour.

The road climbed in elevation and rocky geography appeared, so different from the prairie states. Huge potholes strategically placed to entrap tires and cause shock absorber life warranties to exhaust themselves were the immediate challenges along this well-traveled pavement. Deep into dusk, one of those tractor-trailer dudes sidled up, honked repeatedly, and urgently flashed a handwritten paper in the middle of his right passenger-side window before blowing past. Sheets of rain made his sign hard to decipher, and he and his Kenworth were soon out of sight. I couldn't make heads or tails of what that was all about, and there was nothing to do except stop and walk around to see that the tires remained inflated, the swaying trailer was still hitched, and no taillights had malfunctioned.

Bone-chilling shivers were what I mostly experienced, parked as I was along the roadside in the cold New Mexico spring rain. Temperatures were dropping at an alarming rate, and the isolated, black stretches of New Mexico highway began to resonate with an ominous feeling as darkness fell. Small towns and turn-offs followed one after the other. Where to stop? Through the downpour and encroaching fog, the sign for Santa Rosa was almost missed. Inner instincts screamed, "Stop! Stop! Stop!" Bedding down in Santa Rosa for the night was a split-second decision.

As I was tired to the point of numbness, the night's rest stop seemed particularly short. The next morning, strawberry pancakes suddenly assumed a chokehold position somewhere around my larynx at overhearing banter in the Silver Moon Restaurant.

Chatter was about the unexpected snow and ice storm and how many roads were impassible. That must have been what the truck driver was attempting to convey. Over plain white ceramic mugs of stout coffee, travel-related horror stories were being traded faster than junk bonds. As for my appetite, the food remained on the breakfast plate. I distinctly recollect pausing at the restaurant's cash register on my way out and seeing it flanked with a pencil bouquet of silvery, almond-eyed space aliens. The register's *cha-ching* made their little heads bob wildly. This was Roswell territory. Did they have a message for me?

A decision was made to head cautiously down the road towards Albuquerque rather than to wait it out in Santa Rosa. Highway salt crews had been out, so it was the right decision in retrospect. As we started another climb in elevation, the spectacle of cars plowed into ditches and a jackknifed semi in the median meant that Santa Rosa had been our sole protector through the night. Pristine snow was everywhere across the landscape after we left Santa Rosa, and the scene was certainly a gift in the first miles of morning driving. Coaxed by springtime moisture, the desert floor was carpeted in mossy-green growth, with snow, like cupcake icing, coating the tops of the sagebrush and cacti. What made this moment simply postcard perfect was spotting a fleet-footed pronghorn buck and his harem pawing through the snow for food.

Trust your instincts. When you absolutely need a haven, a Santa Rosa will come into sight.

Prologue

The privilege of establishing a Tucson retirement home has not gone unappreciated, particularly in the moments I spend glancing through my Spanish-style arched windows towards the Santa Catalina Mountains. I have had to release much along this Tucson trek, with its physical, spiritual, and emotional twists. It has not been particularly easy.

As for an olive—well, those little salty morsels I'm finding and savoring in the most unusual places in my new life. Ah, here's to Tucson, with an olive and twist!

Chapter 2: 41 Breakstone Drive

Stories about home and a place in the heart

41 Breakstone Drive

I didn't want to purchase 41 Breakstone Drive, but Sam did. It was obvious that no one had cared for it in quite some time, and there were also issues of mixed-use zoning. In the end, however, it was about tax breaks and office space. It was mostly an impersonal decision.

The Tenant

Loud grinding gravel under hulking Mercedes whitewall tires disturbed the waterfront estate's morning ambience. Bulleting down the mile-long driveway, the Madame sent Canada geese, squirrels, and rabbits in crisscrossed, confused directions. Then, as if the Biblical parting seas had rejoined, morning tranquility once again rolled back across the estate when the towering iron gates closed behind her. Luckily, the estate's flora and fauna were left unscathed. Before long, the automobile had disappeared into a deep distance, and the waterfowl and small creatures resumed their breakfast foraging. Heavens, she was late for her hairdresser appointment at a salon in the vicinity of 41 Breakstone Drive!

We had bought the property at 41 Breakstone Drive as an investment through one of those friend-of-a-friend deals. Sam and I were comfortable middle class, but this certainly saddled us with financial risk we had not previously expected. I had more misgivings about the property and its kludged spaces than my other half. I distinctly remember touring the property immediately after signing choking stacks of mortgage papers. We were indeed committed, with a couple of inherited commercial lessees and a vacant apartment space.

That is when we began to see the property's real blemishes. Its cement was cracking. Water stains hovered like benign spirits, outlined on the walls behind the built-in bookshelves. All the outside stairways also had to be replaced. Our purchase was most assuredly an act of faith, a test of endurance and will. We quickly came to the realization that renovation would take considerable time and money. However, with a little initial fix up, we quietly celebrated Sam's move into his new office space.

We also knew that rental income from the apartment would be essential, so our discussions immediately focused on how best to advertise for a decent tenant. We were instantaneous, over-particular landlords, but up went the "For Rent" sign. The response we got was quite unexpected. It was much to our astonishment when a diminutive, fifty-something woman parked a Mercedes in the driveway and asked to see the apartment. Sam did not accompany her, but he noticed that she remained a very long time before returning downstairs with the keys.

"I'll take it!" she said.

Like some creature detecting threatening scents in the winds, Sam just stood there in stunned silence. She hadn't even asked the rental price.

"This will be short term, and I refuse to sign a contract."

His thousand and one questions got swallowed in the quiet that followed. She shyly smiled.

"Agreed?"

Sam's answer came automaton-like.

"Yes."

I now know that in the two effected households, news of their oral contract was received with the same amount of perturbation. "You did *what*?" That evening, a fog of sullenness rolled over both homes for very different reasons.

Christine's moving day from the estate to our building saw a modest lineup in the driveway, with two vehicles at parade rest until the iron gates opened. Chockfull of boxes, her Mercedes led the way, followed by a rather rickety local, white-painted moving truck. As her stay was to be temporary, most of what she brought was only from her bedroom and personal sitting room. The old Spanish gardener leaned into this rake as he witnessed the gates gradually shut behind the rather strange entourage. His gut feeling was that this estate would never be quite the same again, even when the always-coiffed and stylish Mrs. Christine decided to return.

Another pair of eyes was on Christine's car as she pulled beyond the gates. During the morning moving activities, Don's military training had kept him stoic, like some inanimate toy soldier. With the closing of the gates, he sought refuge in his library, keeping company with his crumbling heart. Christine's announced departure left a chill within the opulence of their home. His gut had told him he would face this situation at some time. Now was that time. As Christine's husband, Don knew he must let go if he ever hoped to hold her again.

But he missed her already.

* * *

At 41 Breakstone Drive, Christine most appreciatively noticed the apartment's sun-drenched living room this first morning away from the estate. She sat cross-legged and mesmerized among her unpacked boxes. There, across the sea foam green carpeting and patterned wallpaper, crept spectacular patterns of light through the louvered shutters. Morning coffee had never been more delicious.

That was it!

Light was one of the absences from her life, she realized as she was momentarily drawn back to the estate house she had temporarily left. Shrouded throughout in European tapestries, its interior was dark and masculine. It was Don's tastes, not hers. Christine now recollected the cinnamon drapery swaying across expansive, leaded windowpanes, as though its only purpose was to shunt sunlight away. Hers was a feeling of emptiness. Over the years, much had been lost in their life together. Don's life was wrapped in his businesses and collections to the point of obsession. Truly, for some time there had been considerable loneliness and separateness under that estate roof.

Christine's apartment was not about running from Don, but rather about renewing herself. It was something she absolutely had to do. As Christine sat in the morning light with her sweats on and her wiry, auburn-streaked hair tamed into a chignon, she felt her stomach quickly knot with uncertainty. How vulnerable and unprotected she suddenly felt, residing on the other side of the estate gates. This was totally impulsive and she felt she should rush home immediately. Don would forgive her. However, her inner voices pleaded her to remain.

In a relatively short time, Christine began to savor no longer being cloistered behind the estate's iron gates. However, her wayfaring was deeply introspective, and, we surmised, somewhat emotionally painful. Curiously, it was her acrylic nails that were the most visible evidence of a deeper, internal shedding process. In meeting Christine, our eyes were immediately drawn to her perfectly manicured hands tipped in deep-colored enamels with exotic names like, "Cappuccino" and "Forbidden Ruby." During her stay in the apartment, she divested herself of these artificial nails as well as many of her other expensive cosmetics.

Christine turned into a voracious learner. She had never cooked, so Sam taught her the basics. She also adored plants and wanted to learn about growing them. She could be found at the apartment's kitchen table in her pink, patterned garden gloves with potting soil spread over her and everything else. She had no idea what it meant for a plant to be root bound, but she found herself having an absolutely wonderful time.

During her stay in the apartment, both Christine and Don remained on amicable terms. There was even an occasional movie and dinner date. After all, this was a temporary arrangement. The winter holiday season came and went, and yet Christine remained at 41 Breakstone Drive. However, we fully expected to be renting the apartment to a new tenant by spring.

It was two springs later that a tearful Christine descended the apartment stairs to announce she was moving back to the estate. Don had become gravely ill. Although Sam and I had frequently discussed among ourselves when Christine would leave, we were not prepared for her departure. By that time there was a genuine friendship between us all, and once she was behind those iron estate gates, we instinctively knew those bonds of friendship would fade.

Sam and I dragged our heels for the rest of the month and didn't advertise the apartment in hopes Christine would change her mind. As we worked around the property on several early mornings, we half expected to hear a moving van rumbling up the back alley with her possessions in tow. Sadly, that day never came.

Christine returned to the estate very much changed. We hear from her occasionally and understand the drapes she so despised have been completely pulled down, and the walls have been splashed with new coats of pastel paint that she personally selected. Christine professes that there are plants growing everywhere there is sunlight. Even with Don being so ill, they now seem to be enjoyably sharing more time together. Interestingly enough, the acrylic nails and makeup were reapplied, as if to protect a fragile, unadorned woman that she simply could not share. Sam and I look at each other and understand it is about light and joy finally penetrating both of their lives.

I think she carried much of the warmth of that apartment back home with her. It was difficult to re-rent Christine's apartment because her presence seemed to linger, but we eventually did.

About all that can memorably be said concerning the succession of tenants following her at 41 Breakstone Drive is that they generally paid their rent on time. While showing the apartment to a prospective tenant, Sam and I both imagined that a whiff of Christine's Oscar de la Renta followed us down the hallway.

The Inveigler

"Inveigler" seems a peculiar term to use, but it fits the situation. Oftentimes when we're working around the property, its physical structure appears as this wonderfully mature woman only in need of cosmetic touchups to keep her looking stunning. She's at her prime! And she's beckoning to us. Other times, when the expenses of renovation mire us, 41 Breakstone Drive appears as a haggard, rouged lady of the night, voraciously consuming us with her constant need for attention and fixes. She's so deceptive. But, somewhere amidst our sweat equity, frustrations, and occasional tears, the property wedged itself deeply into our hearts.

Now Sam and I are mulling over a move to 41 Breakstone Drive, into the apartment that we still consider as Christine's. Perhaps our deepening midlife urges are the real inveigler. Maybe we are only beginning to recognize our aging processes. It's at that very moment when you set about, with a great sense of urgency and some blindness, simplifying your life. Suddenly it's time to prepare for growing older.

I was determined that planning for the move to 41 Breakstone Drive would be done systematically. Every month would have its schedule of sorting, throwing out, and packing. And, by the way, during this process Sam and I would also gracefully face into the winds of our next decade together. All of this would be a sort of controlled, smooth transition into the next phase of our lives.

Ironically, our rites of passage had nothing to do with us physically preparing for the move to 41 Breakstone Drive. A sudden death in our immediate family was an awakening. In retrospect, it was as if this purging were our payment for ultimately reaching our new address and our new life.

Legacy of the Ogon

Over time our commercial lessees changed, and we made the decision to move into the apartment at 41 Breakstone Drive. Our attention then turned from maintenance to enhancing our investment. We would sometimes sit, tired and sweaty from chores, on one of the crumbling brick retainer walls that girded our property. What needed to be done was endless and overwhelming. To the side of the moss-encrusted privacy fencing was a deck housing the worst eyesore on the property—a dilapidated hot tub. Dried leaves had covered a portion of the tub's torn, maroon vinyl cover. Appropriately, the tub was guarded by a rust-hinged gate. Then, as we sat there one evening, a vision came to us about creating a wonderful city garden.

How preposterous to think we could sleep! Landscaping ideas were firing from all corners of our imaginations, and by morning sketches and several cups of cold tea were strewn across our dining room table. Among the mess of papers lingered our initial thoughts about an arbor-looking structure and a pond.

With the inception of our Japanese garden came the pond and its new residents. There were the orange fantails and a black moor as starter gifts from another pond owner. We were caught by surprise when the contractor who helped us with the pond masonry and pumping systems released two Japanese koi among our first batch of goldfish.

Over the span of a couple of months, in what had been the property's deteriorating hot tub area, incredibly patterned creatures now swam. In the first evening of their arrival, Sam and I rested on cedar benches beside the pond, mesmerized by their grace and beauty. The white koi was generously dappled with red and black markings down its back. Accompanying the white koi as it toured the pond, but much smaller, was a predominately black male koi, which was splotched with white and orange.

Our fascination with the pond soon led us to contact a koi breeder. Walking into the breeder's pond area, we immediately spotted the Ogon hugged against the other fish. It was the koi's creamy white iridescence and absence of color patterns that caught our eyes.

* * *

The Ogon felt transparent and sheltered. Surely they would not be after her. Now a bit panicky, she maneuvered herself deeper towards the center of the pond and froze. Her senses locked onto an eerie, threatening stillness. Motionlessness seized hold of the pond.

* * *

Sam and my shadowy figures hovered above her. "That one!"

* * *

The pan net surreptitiously enmeshed her! Suddenly feeling the netting, her curving dorsal fin went rigid. She was slowly pulled towards the surface air, and her gill covers began to oscillate wildly. However, it was not the horrific moments of pursuit and seizure that her instincts had communicated as she watched the others being netted. Hers was a quiet, exhausting capture. Her collected energy was exerted into a single, powerful backward thrust to return her to the waters where she had been spawned. But an oxygenated plastic bag had been prepared, and after encapsulating her it was quickly cinched.

Sadly, the journey away from her breeding place had begun.

* * *

Sam drove, and I nursed the oxygenated bag all the way back to 41 Breakstone Drive. Following the breeder's instruction, we floated the bag on top of our pond for an hour and a half to adjust both water temperatures. The evening arbor lights had just clicked on when we both ceremoniously knelt beside the pond to release her. Even with the bag open and the pond waters washing over her, the Ogon remained absolutely still. We nudged the bag. She did not move.

After a minute or so, there was still no movement from us or from the koi. A crescent moon now illuminated the edges of night clouds. Exhausted, we were caught in a waiting game. In the sultry evening stillness, the Ogon suddenly moved, startling us. Her tail fin slapped hard against the side of the plastic bag, and her rippling muscles propelled her deep into the pond. For an instant we lost sight of her. Then she resurfaced with moonlight capturing the beauty of her yellowish-white scales. The Ogon's dorsal fin fanned regally upwards, and her mouth tipped slightly out of the water to expose elongated front barbels.

It was quite evident that the matriarch of our pond had arrived.

We managed to successfully nurse all of our pond's finned residents through a rather mild winter of occasional snowfalls. Twice we had to chip away ice to assure that the state of torpor in our fish remained undisturbed. The snow-encrusted Japanese winter garden with its Tachi-gata stone lanterns was a spectacle we enjoyed over steaming green tea.

The El Niño-driven winter had induced an unusually warm spring and early summer. With the danger of frost passing, our matriarchal Ogon would push up to the surface and leisurely feed among the water plants. By June, the summer weather hovered at insufferably humid upper ninety-degree levels. Sam and I had our hands full ensuring that the pond's filtration system kept oxygen and carbon dioxide levels in balance. We also sensed that the unusually hot weather had severely disrupted the spawning season. The summer already seemed interminable.

Just when we had dismissed hopes of offspring from any of the fish, including the majestic Ogon, the water temperature and a full moon aligned one particular late June evening. At dawn the next day, we watched the askew water hyacinths bobbing like corks and fish zooming through the darkened, frothy water. Laced with millions of eggs, our pond was anything but calm. The pond eventually regained its equilibrium as nature took its course. The mature fish devoured newly laid eggs, and only the hardiest of the fry survived. Predators also came in the form of a crow-sized green heron and city-dwelling raccoons conducting nocturnal skirmishes. Amazingly, of the twenty or so new fish that ultimately survived, six were the Ogon's offspring. Her metallic, creamy white coloring was passed to this new generation.

Around Father's Day the following spring, Sam was awaiting his early morning airport shuttle. As he went to feed the pond's creatures in the daybreak light, he was shocked to discover the Ogon struggling to spawn in the shallow side of the pond. She appeared to be having extreme difficulties. All that Sam could do was telephone me as his ride honked impatiently in the driveway. He had to go, and I was alone. I felt a real sense of relief in the evening to see our pond fairly calm. The Ogon was quietly resting in water that was darker than usual and laced with a frothy scum. Eggs were clustered everywhere under the plants. What was unusual was the noticeable lethargy that had crept over all the pond's inhabitants. None of them came to the surface to feed. That evening I sat beside our pond for a good hour and a half, mostly to assure myself that all was in order. What else could I do? Bone tired, I then went to bed.

Sam called very late. All I could say was that everything looked okay. It wasn't.

Running late the next morning, I opened the first garden gate and hurriedly moved down the brick path to the second wooden gate. With a thousand of the day's "to-do" things on my mind, I pushed the second gate open and traveled across the wooden deck, only to abruptly halt in mid step—the Ogon's whiteness against the water's surface immediately drew my eye. There she was, lifelessly floating among the plants. The whole pond appeared eerily still. I simply could not believe we had lost this magnificent specimen, and my throat closed tightly. Sometime after late evening the day before, our Ogon's breath of life had quietly been extinguished. For just a fleeting second, my mind envisioned a thousand points of candlelight being snuffed into darkness. Are all our departures so unheard, as was the Ogon's, in the life-death cycle we are inevitably a part of?

I felt weak and missed Sam very much.

Life in the pond eventually readjusted without its first matriarch. Curiously, one of the Ogon's yellow, metallic-colored offspring, with its bright orange circular marking on its head, took her place beside our largest male koi.

On those special autumn evenings when the air becomes cooler than the earth, we sit spellbound in our Japanese garden. It is a spiritual time, as the fog stealthily wends its way upland and turns toward 41 Breakstone Drive. You can actually see it blanket the pond. Sam and I remain convinced that our Ogon's spirit travels with the fog. To this very day, she remains in guardianship of this special place on earth.

The Departure

The next decade of our lives was good to us at 41 Breakstone Drive. Move away from there? Never! Well, "never say never" is one of those extremely hard-to-learn life lessons. For a number of reasons and with very heavy hearts, Sam and I did eventually sell the property, including the Japanese garden and its inhabitants. Coincidentally, a series of house mishaps occurred in the days leading up to closing the sale. It was as if the property's life systems were beginning to fray at their peripheries and the energy of the house was subtly slipping into failure mode.

Emblazoned on my soul until the day I die will be my final look over my shoulder at the dark, spiritless windows of our now vacant building. All Sam and I could do was suck in our breath, head down the back alley, and hit the open road to the rest of our life—all done with a great deal of apprehension and uncertainty. We instinctively knew that 41 Breakstone Drive could never be replaced.

Chapter 3: I Don't Have Time to Plant Small Trees

Poetry and stories about beating time

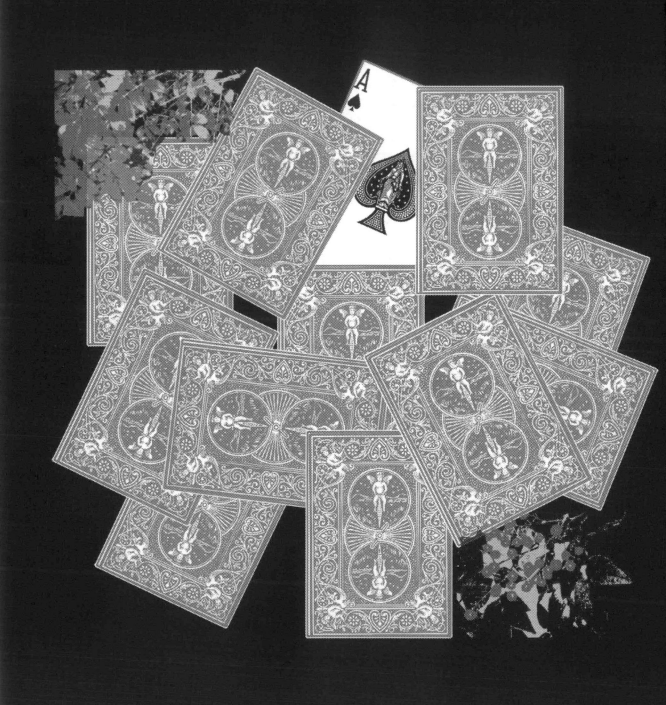

The Parlor Game

It certainly is a pleasurable paradox sitting in this turn-of-the-century Victorian parlor, with its overstuffed, horsehair furniture and high, ornate ceilings, at my mid-life point and postured for celebrating the new millennium. Our host has made today's parlor games captivating.

Now it's my turn.

Cupped in hand like a veritable treasure, the cards are laid before me. What I notice first are the intricate drawings of a garden, presented in a magnificent combination of the four seasons. Spring is arrayed in subtle yellow and lilac tones; the summer garden cards are splashed with bold sunflowers and nude cupid statuary. Autumn is dressed in burnt orange and magenta. Most intriguing are the winter cards in muted grays with their laboriously snow-bent tree silhouettes.

Next, I turn and fan the deck, face up. What illusion is this?

I am bedazzled as everything and everyone in the room abruptly fade away. It is as if each of the cards is a miniature holograph of the years and events of my life. I begin slowly but am soon frantic in ordering and moving the playing cards across the marble tabletop and into discernable patterns.

The card arrangements become blurred. I simply cannot find meaning in the patterns I have created. I squirm and then reorder the cards, smearing them around the table in a panic.

I *must* do something, and quickly. I feel submerged, sickened, and breathless. My eyes sense the pressure of imploding, dizzying blackness. I am losing. Everything in my gut lurches as I try in these moments to make sense of my life. I briefly notice that my host and fellow guests are offering little support. Is it that my raging inquietude is invisible to them?

At that very moment, I become transfixed by the small garden outside of the parlor window. It somehow becomes my medium. With a degree of returning composure, I begin to interpret this most curious set of playing cards. It's really not important as to what specific explanations I offer myself through studying the variations and patterns of these cards. The card backs, with their seasonal garden drawings, ended up on the table considerably interspersed.

I'm sure this scattering of cards indicates that my winter tide gardens were mostly experienced when I was in my twenties. It was my decade of hollowness, of seeking, and of almost surrendering to the dark, suicidal urges.

It is also reassuring the richly hued summertime and fall garden cards have collected nearest to me, for I am now very busy and involved with the rhythms and complexities of living.

Unexpectedly, the penetration of masculine whispering brings me through to consciousness. It is our host who leans over me.

"The cards, please!"

In their being passed along, I notice a kind of metamorphosis of the card deck into new colors and designs for the next player. The only card which remains the same for all parlor guests is the Face-o'-Death card. We are blessed with luck that no one has played that card yet today.

Now it's your turn.

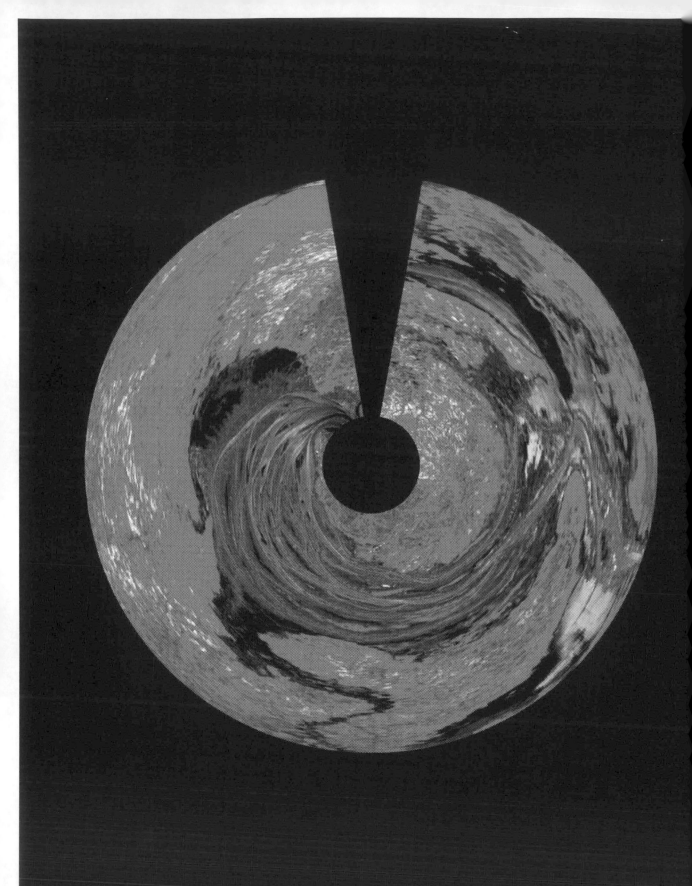

The Weaver

In the beginning
were raging seas of fire
spinning molten strands
into the fabric of our universe.

Millenniums of interconnected souls
textured by angry pools of
purplish black war
and mankind's indiscretions.

Is the weaver spellbound
by the topology of this never-ending creation?
Explosions of individual lives
color his intricate patterns.

I am not gifted, as are others, with
the weaver's sense of vision.

For I am too busy mending
what death has suddenly
and personally torn
from me.

Remembering

Today, I rise as always ahead of the household, just to experience early morning outside. Even if my private sojourn outdoors means that I'm tucked under an umbrella, it's a journey I *very much* anticipate.

Like some giant oval egg cracking through the night's cloud cover, the sun is fast spilling daybreak through the trees and onto our lawn. Barefooted, I smoothly and quietly close the back screen door behind me. With a coffee cup in my hand, there is a sense of quiet urgency in my shuffling across the gray-stained deck. I must hurry if I wish to have this new daylight bathe my face and witness it around the crowded, blooming plants.

Perching on the step landing, I reflect to myself, "I'm here, again, for yet another time!" At that moment the regal Charlie's White Peonies capture my eye. Their allure is as a time machine, transporting me back to the 1950s.

There I am sleepily toddling along beside my mother. This is the morning for her to be in her garden, quietly snipping away at her peonies and iris. I envision her wearing a sleeveless, cotton print housedress, cinched with the dutifully matching belt. Her matronly form hunches over the bucketful of blossoms she has gathered from along the fence lines in the predawn. We disturb the dampened, clover-spiked grass and send a cottontail bolting along the railroad tracks. Then, in her soft-spoken manner, Mom tells me it's time to go.

Off to the cemetery we steer in her Chevrolet Two-Ten.

Not a soul would be there at that early hour. One could hear the distant highway sounds as Mom and I picked our way through the evergreens to the family plot. It was always my job to clean out the vases and prepare them for the new flowers.

When the flowers were clipped and carefully arranged, our tasks were finished. Then this kind of deadly silence would shroud us, as just Mom and I seemingly hovered over the family's granite grave markers. As a child, none of the etched names were a part of my life, and it was difficult for me to understand Mom's yearly ritual. However, I sensed it was special and something she desperately wanted to share with me.

What I mostly recollect was seeing, in the first light of day, tears travel down Mom's rouged cheeks. She would squeeze my small hand as if it were some special signal that everything was done. That would be that, and as if on cue we would crawl back into the sedan. We always rode the return trip in silence, wending our way back through the massive wrought-iron cemetery gates, heading home just after daybreak.

I have only a few more treasured moments to myself on our back deck before the Memorial Day hoopla begins and voices from within the house banish my ritual of remembering and loving. I'm living a thousand miles from the old family plot. Even when I wire for a floral wreath, I'm never really sure it looks okay, or, for that matter, if it ever got placed properly on my mother's grave.

I sense that today's younger, urban-centered generations are much more removed from trips to cemeteries and harboring thoughts of being silent and reflective. I guess that's okay. Maybe decorating graves is just plain old fashioned and should fade with my generation. Maybe the kindness of a passerby will bear an occasional iris or peony to our family plot long after I'm gone. Maybe. My eyes briefly moisten.

I find it very difficult to physically lift myself up from the stoop on such a resplendent Memorial Day morning. So, I linger on.

"What's for breakfast?"

The immediacy of voices abruptly drills through my head, which has been lost in thoughts of long ago. But I quickly unfold myself and rise. It's time to go back inside.

Being There

Scuttling through
germicide-scented
corridors
I find myself at
a dead end
confined by a
glassed-in room
pressing me
face to face
with *them*.

In groups of four,
and two,
they are like ancient
alien beings
sitting rigid, without
conversation,
staring past each
other.

Duty bound, we come
ritualistically
to this colorless,
medicinal place
only to witness
consecutive
sameness.

They
are as mannequins
with a succession
of screw-like faces;
as one disappears,
another replaces.

Today,
a country-woman's vacant,
    blue-veined face
framed in
Buster Brown bangs
with butterfly wisps of
yellowing hair
flying around her ears
mostly
intrigues me.

Prolonged hours are
interrupted
for them
when white towels
lazily draped
about each wrinkled,
sagging-chinned neck
means
spoon-feeding
aged loved ones.

Some of *them* drool.

Afterwards,
attempting to clear
my head,
I hurriedly bear down
on my gas pedal
exiting the parking lot
recollecting a thousand
errands of life's
busyness
not yet done.

I surmise
they
have been
where
I am
now.

Briefly glimpsing my
image in the
rearview mirror
assures me of my
fortyish–fiftyish
vitality
guarding against ever
having to
be there.

Not me!

Such false reassurance!

Deep down
I know that
and
my auto
picks up
speed
for there is so much
remaining
that
I
must
do.

The China Pattern

When I cleaned out my mother's house, in the back of her china cabinet I found three or four cups and saucers and a couple salad plates. I just packed them without another thought. That was almost ten years ago.

I don't know why, but I recently looked at the bottom shelf of my breakfront, and there they were, stacked and coated with dust. Kind of haunting, really. Lenox stopped their "Fanciful" dinnerware pattern around 1985. I know that my mother inherited these odds and ends from her older sister—my mother was never the fancy kind, but her sister definitely was.

Briefly, I wonder if there was once a complete set. And, if I listen closely, I can almost hear the holiday chatter reverberating across this china which must have sumptuously dressed every holiday dinner table.

Perhaps I am searching for more fullness in my own life. I have set about acquiring several place settings with the help of antique dealers across the country. In fact, it's a personal passion of sorts. My mother's spirit must be smiling on this '60s blue jeans and pottery girl.

Now, I wonder whose cabinet this completed collection will rest in after mine. Maybe it is just a girl thing to think about this kind of stuff.

Epiphany

Introspection over coffee
is the pleasure of this
rainy November daybreak;
as morning light tempts my eyes
through windowpane reflections
to tidal marshes circled by
an Indian summer's hued leaves.

Nature's quintessential
celebration of living!
Magenta-rust-yellow-orange
transformations
to sepia dissolving into
colorlessness;
ultimately into decay;
a variegated palette from
which other life will
surely come.

I sense, full well,
my abounding mid-life years
beginning to feel slight aches;
turning earthwards; and,
better understand autumn trees
hunkering
against approaching winter.

There's now an urgency
to time spent;
discovering hints of finality
in one's own breath of life.

Before the northern wind
spirals me as it would
lingering foliage
down and down
into nature's inevitable
decay/regeneration cycle,
what must I capture
as a window to my soul,
for others to build on, or,
more simply,
merely to be
remembered by?

To leave no earthly
trace of self
becomes
unthinkable!

Is that vanity?

For me,
it's the most perplexing
of mid-life questions.

The Piano

It belonged to my dream. The baby grand piano, made of walnut, consumed hard-earned dollars from my first real job. The piano was something I simply just had to possess. In my reflections, the piano actually must have looked quite silly in the series of cramped apartments and townhouses that became my lifestyle.

That dream began well over thirty-some years ago.

I knew that eventually there would be a spacious living room in which to house it. As it continued to be my special dream, my piano was religiously trucked with me in all my many moves. However, the suburbs and split-level house, complete with dog, never came. That's just a fact, stated with little, if any, regret. But, in the richness of my life's twists and turns, that exquisite piano has always been there, serving as a sort of anchor to my young, idealistic woman's dreams.

Recently, in the middle of the night, I abruptly awakened to intruding thoughts about being on the verge of my fifties. It's certainly not a comfortable feeling, and it made me sweat profusely.

Now I'm experiencing a real sense of losing both balance and security in my life. It's as if a sort of obscuring fog has sidled up rudely and announced its engulfment of my very soul. With such thoughts come almost primeval urges to do something—anything—radically different.

Surprising even to myself, my very first action was to call piano dealers. It was done almost mechanically. After two or three contacts, a diminutive, white-haired gentleman in a maroon sweater arrived quietly at my door and offered a fair price. In less than a half hour, my long-time dream was his possession.

So what's the big deal about getting rid of a piano?

Very simply, at fifty, it's time to divest of *things* in my life. It's time to get rid of clutter and years of collecting. It's also time to refocus on what is most important to me in my remaining earthly years. In each of our own distinct ways, we all undergo this journey. As for that piano, it's where I personally chose to begin. It's at the very heart of my early dreams—and now those dreams are crowding me.

The Vigil

This is the first
I have studied my father
as a new widower,
extricated
from responsibilities
of constantly
nurturing others.

Observing him intently,
couched there,
in late afternoon shadows,
I *finally* understand
him allowing me
to come
and go
so freely
through my growing years;
rebellious
self-absorbed years
consumed with
wounds of the heart.

I am his daughter;
but he,
the greater lifetime
of my experiences.

Foolishly, I have always
thought myself
the far more
sagacious and worldly
one!

It is in accompanying
him through this private vigil
that I now realize
how terribly wrong I am.

His manhood,
a life of vast richness,
provides
inner strength he
now draws on,
smiling ever so faintly,
looking forward
through
his tears.

Could I do likewise?
I suspect not.

The Paradise Flea Market

Returning to Eastern Standard Time from a remote Pacific island time zone has created mixed senses of exhilaration, swirling with a bone-tired emptiness of sorts. There are the obligatory souvenirs, journaling notes, and ticket stubs to make it all seem more real. Memories can be summoned at a word.

But now it's really the hodgepodge of photos spread across the dining room table for weeks at a time that I must contend with. What to do with them? It's becoming increasingly bothersome. Lordy, there's an overabundance of photo albums in this house already!

I feel my toes twist and curl in resistance to the thought of organizing them. A bad investment in time, I think. Maybe I'm simply tired of photographs. Even ten years after closing my parent's home, dusty boxes of photos still remain in the back of a downstairs closet in my house. I cannot bring myself to deal with this family collection. Now there's the thought about what, if anything, these inanimate pieces of paper do for us. Nothing really, I guess.

My frustration finds me on an excursion deep into the closet, hunting a spare box. I will get them out of sight and then make excuses both to others and to myself. As I make bold, cleaning sweeps across the cluttered dining room table, the one which drops to the floor is a white, jacketed 3" x 4" photo. I knew better than to open it, but I did.

All the sensuousness of the Paradise Flea Market was immediately conjured up once more. It's a place of exotic-faced hucksters and blended camellia-coconut-lilikoi lotion smells. Its breeze-blown, vibrantly colored sarongs beckon with a kind of spirituality, which invites total envelopment. The tropical sun and accompanying trade winds assure the taste of ocean salt across licked lips.

The market is a place of intoxication. It is where time seems suspended and money has relatively little value, except in exchange for trinkets, which are won mostly through haggling. Money exchanges are also the most fragile of commodities. In the hint of sunset and the approach of cooling evening sea breezes, the market quickly folds in on itself. Like the magnificent, sun-loving hibiscus bloom, the Paradise Flea Market silently disappears with the night winds, scattering its remnants far and wide.

Racks and racks of colorful island clothing attract my eye. There are garments in blue and sea foam green combinations; those in calming, cool white tones; and those in black, bearing bold, brownish Tahitian petroglyphs. Wrinkled and crammed into a tiny corner of the market stall, I am attracted to a brilliantly fused vermilion and fuchsia garment with intriguing black fish swimming across its weaves.

"I'll take that one!"

"Sold!"

I struggle to put away my thoughts and rid my dining room table of this vacation clutter. However, the photo proves too hypnotic and quickly lures me back to that marketplace.

Images of the redheaded, pale-skinned shop lady are instantly evoked. Wheelchair bound, she sits alone and away from the market cacophony. Her stall is nondescript. We pass her a couple times and go about our shopping, as there certainly aren't any bright-hued island colors to attract the eye to her wares. She sits shrouded in the simplest of makeshift, black fabric tents. What could she possibly be selling? That is when our eyes make contact. She is selling aura readings.

"How much?"

"Twenty dollars."

I guess it was more curiosity than anything else which ultimately made me put my money down on her literature-strewn table. I'm certainly not into all that metaphysical mumbo jumbo. I know she sensed that as she asked me in a very quiet voice to breathe deeply and calm myself. How did she know that my anxiety was heightening? I felt qualmishness fuel my regrets for even getting into this situation—and in a flea market, of all places!

Oh well.

My thoughts were to just get quickly on with this reading. At that moment I felt rather foolish in front of market passersby, with each of my hands strapped to metal-plated, boxlike contraptions. At least no one knew me. There I sat, just waiting for electrophysiological principles to work their magic. My aura photograph was being developed.

The wait seemed interminable to me. I used my time to study this purveyor of aura readings. What I most noticed were her bare feet. Unclipped toenails curled into the worn, yellowing foam-rubber padding at the base of her wheelchair. There was also a peculiar brilliance to her Egyptian-character gold bracelet.

As for what came next, I was simply not prepared.

As she gingerly pealed back the photographic developing paper, I noticed my face surrounded en masse by the identical vermilion and fuchsia colors of the dress I had purchased not over an hour ago. I knew she could not have seen this garment, scrunched as it was below other flea market treasures deep inside an opaque plastic bag. Yet, revealed now, swirling about my head, were those very same colors!

The serendipity of her soothing voice, as my interpreting guide, and the scents of the Paradise Market were now intermingling to make me increasingly light-headed. My laughs went weak and nervous, as I dared not let her see her affect on me. It was as if she were suddenly my spiritual pathfinder, painstakingly peeling back the layers of my innermost thoughts and soul. At midlife it is extremely uncomfortable to become noiseless and hear voices from within.

That aura reading was my moment of catharsis. Tears began to flow.

After a few moments of silence, I detected that we were both extremely tired. Our session was finished. I departed from her booth, aura photo in hand, and never looked back. Whether it was really excellent guesswork or her talents were of a truly clairvoyant nature, I will never know. More importantly, it really doesn't matter.

As for my day at the Paradise Flea Market, I discovered more than I ever could have imagined about myself. It was my signpost for realizing what is truly important in the earthly years I have remaining.

I must unclutter my life. I must. I must.

I have now settled back into the grayness of daily routine. However, I often wistfully reflect back on my Paradise Flea Market experience and the richness of what it revealed to me --all quite unexpectedly. Now, I'm wondering how many Paradise Flea Markets present themselves in each of our lives that we blindly and skeptically pass by, just too reluctant or too unbelieving to really examine.

Broken Dreams

You just can't dwell
in broken dreams
like some vacated house
hunched
in stillness and disrepair
where the past echoes
against smudged walls
and each of us stumble over
innermost thoughts like
frayed carpeting edged
in the middle of your mind.

You must eradicate
or
you must rebuild!

To pause in such
broken dreams
is to surely die away.

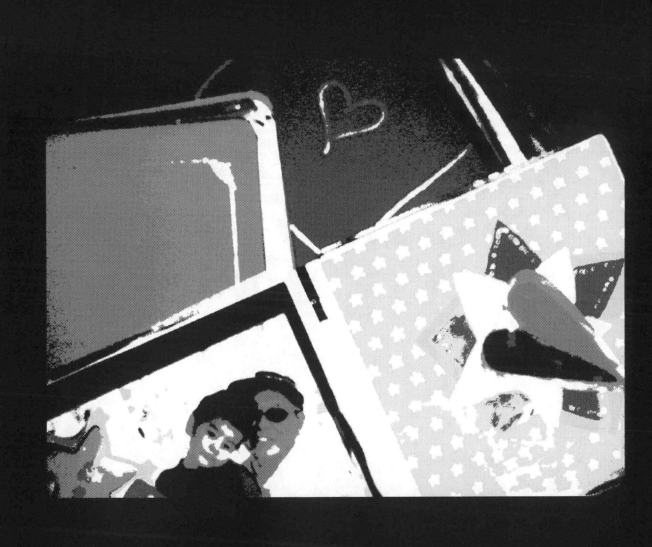

The Scrapbook

You grow up
Get married
Raise your own
And survive and love
The whole life process
       With its attending heart breaks
       joys
       stresses
       and worries
       peppered with rare
       moments of feeling really good
For much has been accomplished
Just in living
Everyday
and coping.

Kids leave.
Home becomes empty.
Pursuing their busy lives,
They're all grown up now.

Then, it happens
The gift of new lives
Next generations
To watch
To absorb
And to take delight in.

Chapter 4: Hearts in Two-Step

Poetry about the entanglement of hearts

Introspective

Some days you are with me,
Some days, not at all;

As this evening when I sip cocktails
And hold court over
Dusky candle shadows devouring
One another on my walls.

Compelled to reason out
Lingering silences which
Deepen between us;

Yet really expecting no answer
From the fluttering shadows
Or from you.

Memorabilia

Remember that waggish
Straw-brimmed hat
I owned?
The going-to-the-beach one?

Brandishing it, you would
Parade around so cavalierly
Imitating me.
Then we would both convulse
In laughter!

Give up this hat
Which cupped my shells and
Other assorted Saturday treasures?
Never!

Well, I reluctantly threw it out today,
Outgrown and patch worn,
After much thought and
Many years later.

Now, I'm wondering
Why I gave you up
So easily
Then.

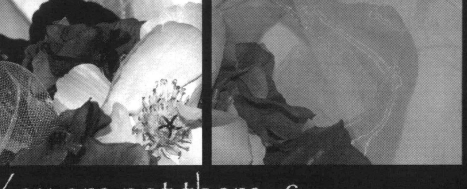

You are not there for me.

Dreambuilder

I misunderstood the meaning
of your dreams
when I ask you questions
about
long-term plans
and
future commitments.

I get a distant response.

You are not ready;
You are not there for me.

What two people in love
build dreams on
is holding each other
at the day's beginning and end.

What two people in love
build dreams on
are conversations with the
staccato of kisses
among the bed linens.

All in anticipation of another
day to spend
together.

Never Just Us!

I
had thought
discovering
my life partner
would be
an orderly,
progressive
process,
with each experience
of being *in love* neatly
building on
the next.

Since
the dark exotics
of our first
impassioned kiss
I
now realize
that such relationships
are really
intervals
of blindly feeling and
groping
along walls,
never knowing
where the next
window or door will lead,
if through our own lives
or, hurtfully, through the lives
of *others*.

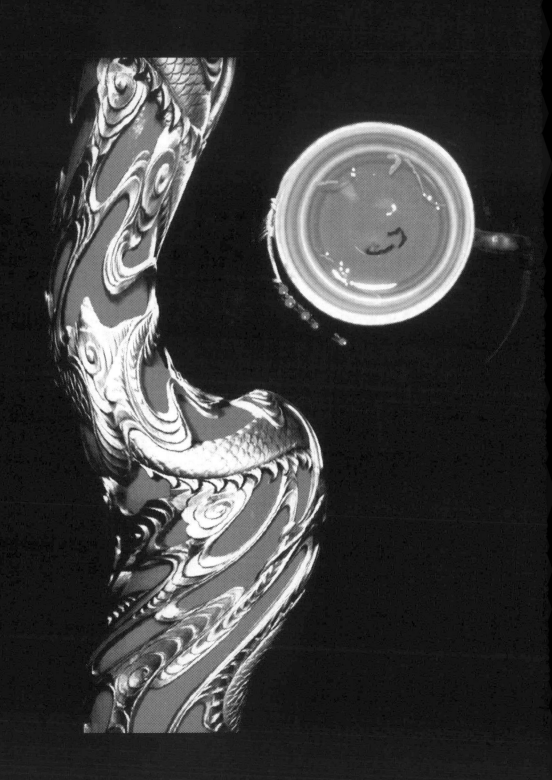

The Serpent Woman

I feel so old and feeble now, sitting in my wicker chair and sipping on the drug-laced tea. I am waiting for him, and remembering. Lately, I turn over and over every facet of my mind's prism of recollections.

Afternoon shadows cavort across my balcony tiles, and a humid, tropical breeze through the foliage constantly rearranges them in different patterns. I have lived in this culture for many, many years. Its rhythms are familiar and comforting. However, the imminence of my final journey back home is very much with me these days. I sense it but do not fear it. My life has been long and vastly rich.

As the old woman in the cramped, upstairs apartment, I've become a legend of sorts in this neighborhood. Children still whisper and giggle when they see me in the street, shuffling about my daily business—if they only knew what I have experienced through my eyes and heart. When I stare into the scratched, darkened bathroom mirror, I only see a young, redheaded woman. There are no wrinkles or telltale age marks to be seen.

The children have undoubtedly heard about the tattoo.

It's a tattoo of a serpent posturing as a magnificent Chinese fire dragon. Even after all these years, the intricacy of its designs and colors still undulate with my every muscle movement. Of course, my clothes cover all, but the serpent's tail which is entwined artfully about my neck.

I don't know how the stranger traced my whereabouts and delivered the letter to me. And, when I agreed to this meeting, he also relayed my hand-penned reply. Now I sit in anticipation and reverie as the narcotics in my tea suddenly bring you so very clearly back from death to me. Briefly, we are together again.

We traveled across continents. I still ache for your arms and touch, and my ears continue to hear you laugh and cry. All our years together were of strengthening love and fulfillment. The serpent tattoo was your idea, brought to life by an old Philippine artist. The serpent's rhythms were our intimate secret.

The knock comes abruptly, intruding on my thoughts. In an instant, you are scattered among the late-afternoon shadows. The expected visitor's handsomeness takes my breath away as he moves cautiously through the door and into my space. With his youthfulness and clearly American style, he precisely honors our appointment time. It is also there, deep within his eyes—his father's passion for living.

I hesitate.

Then, he puts me more at ease with his evident excitement about being here. It's obvious he wants to explore his father's past through me. We share a world of recollections over the amenities of tea and sweets that afternoon. It is inevitable that our conversation eventually turn to the serpent tattooed on my body. That is when our talking stopped and the silence became awkward as we watched the sun melt into its evening hues.

In that moment we both instinctively know what needs to remain unstated and sense this is the close of our visit. Our words and thoughts are carefully folded and then tucked neatly away. He lightly busses my cheek, turns, and starts down the steps from my apartment door.

I want to impulsively call after him and divulge the very secrets of my tattoo. I will disclose the deep passion I felt for his father. I will hug him and wish for him a Serpent Woman! Instead, I merely stand there for a very long time in tearful, empty silence.

How can I possibly take the wonderful details of our love to my grave? How can I not share?

Regrettably, I do nothing.

Into Night's Dangers

What are you doing, girlfriend,
mascaraed, primping,
and anticipating tonight?

Let's walk to the dock's end
and think awhile.

Are you grasping for
what has been lost
between husband and wife?

Your creative fires
grow cold, perhaps?

Childlike, I peek over
the dock's edge
and am startled at
my own reflection
of a woman
ripping through
quiet tides
of being married.

I really don't know her.

Flowing from a husband
to a lover,
I reflect on the sunset
burning tidal marshes
into darkness.

Instinctively, my heart
understands
the marsh heron's sudden
nocturnal screech.

We are both flying blindly and alone,
into night's
dangers.

Social Amenities of Dining

Primeval animal!
Flaring your nostrils
Into courtship's windstorms of sensuality.

Three guests besides you and me
Sit in quiet dinner repartee.

Clever beast!
Our guests do not discern
The quickened hunt.

Three guests besides you and me
Continue to sit in quiet dinner repartee.

Or detect your crouching
Over the fragile wine glass
Being devoured by desire for me!

Parameters

This house absorbs
sequestered,
joyful hours
we've spent together
free from
confining, nagging,
delineating lines
demarcating
our lives
beyond its walls.

Here,
you and I create
preciously different space
each time we're
together.

But,
when you leave,
I close the door
anxiously empty,
just as when I had
first
opened it
to you.

Always wondering.

When will be the time
if ever
you desire
to remain
with me?

Chapter 5: Cat Tales

Stories about cherished feline companions

Butterflies of Summer

I have always loved cats and hope to nurture my multiple-cat household well into my twilight years. These little creatures, each with a distinct personality, have been in constant attendance through my life. Their comings and goings have been of utmost delight, with hints of bittersweet. Yogurt was among my favorites.

In the quiet of being home alone, the butterflies of summer often come back to me. The summer of 1995 was one of slowing my pace. I attribute this to reaching my mid forties. Work was judiciously scheduled so as to have one day per week to spend observing summer unwrap itself. I planted seeds. They flourished, and I was simply delighted. But the best treasure of all was the kaleidoscope of butterflies in their variegated wing patterns parading across my colorful bursts of impatiens. And, of course, keeping me company were my three feline companions, with Yogurt as the senior cat. He was particularly playful in rousting the elusive winged creatures.

In 1986 Yogurt had come to me as a butterfly of chance. Another person's cruelty ultimately resulted in landing the bedraggled kitten in my garage. Two boys on bicycles had spotted slight movement in a tied plastic garbage bag thrown along the country roadside. To their mother's chagrin, they discovered the kitten deep within this bag. "Not another pet!" I surmise was the classic maternal answer. So, the boys set out to find their discovery a home.

The boys' evening bicycling eventually brought them to the last house down the hill, which was mine. Dangling limp by the nape of his neck and, worse yet, appearing at eye level when I opened the door, was a supposedly white kitten. He was dying. The vagaries of fate had certainly not been kind to him. His ears were black and cracked from severe sunburn. His fur had a gray cast and was extremely greasy. Then there was all the host of usual maladies suffered by tiny, abandoned kittens.

I accepted this kitten and for the evening relegated him to the garage with something to eat. Now I had the thankless job of seeing that he not suffer further. Arrangements would have to be made in the morning with the veterinary to put him to sleep, provided he even made it through the night.

With the kitten wrapped in a towel and tucked in a shoebox, the trip to the veterinary was only traumatic for me. The little rascal was purring! That evening I returned home with a creature that had been bathed, dewormed, given shots, and was now accompanied by abundant quantities of salve. The all-white Yogurt, with his very pink ears, had just stepped into my life and would remain for the next decade. My resident gray tabby was certainly not excited by the prospect of sharing with our newcomer, but life soon adjusted around the house. I watched Yogurt mature into a magnificent specimen, with hints of white Angora in his dubious ancestry.

Yogurt's origins will forever remain a mystery. That's okay. What I came to realize in my summer of gardening is that the butterflies of good fortune alight ever so unexpectedly and randomly, making new blossoms possible were you least expect them.

When I look back now, my summer of butterflies was certainly unusual for me. In my twenties and thirties, I looked forward to the next thing and then the next. Upsets fell away at each turn. It was always what was ahead that was of importance to me. As part of the baby-boomer generation, career decisions came easily; calling someplace home and sinking roots did not. Yogurt was there for me throughout this time. Conversations of joy and intimacy have all been whispered in his ears, and that little guy endured more moves crisscrossing this country than I have fingers on one hand. That is how he supported my career.

Between moves, he was shuttled off to Mom's house, complete with toys and his life's security—a hand-woven grapevine basket to curl up in. His unquestioning acceptance of the fate of my career moves earned him his title of nobility, namely, Mr. Humphrey Yogurt! Of course, Mom's sleight-of-hand in feeding Yogurt table morsels also went a long ways to soothing any turbulence in his life.

One of my fondest remembrances of him is with nose pressed against the glass of the front door. The faithful Yogurt was always there to greet me in the many houses we called home. Always. I thought of him as my furry welcome mat.

Mr. H. Yogurt also enjoyed his share of mischief. When my white tornado went pell-mell through the house, he curved his body like a desert sidewinder, with all his fur standing in seeming static shock. I still remember my seventy-something mother recounting Yogurt's dryer episode.

She had inadvertently shut the dryer door with him inside! For the next moments, Yogurt, I'm sure, lost one or more of his nine lives. In the flurry of yells and meows from both human and cat, the dryer door was flung open. My imagination still conjures up a white flurry, as if he were a hovercraft moving just above the ground and slightly below the speed of light. Yogurt had been briefly fluff dried!

My early forties brought me the gift of someone I was truly in love with. Yogurt was the elder statesman in what had now grown into a household of three cats. After my rather turbulent twenties and thirties, our lives settled in. Yogurt's favorite place in what was now a permanent home was the second-floor screened porch, which looked down on our ground-level deck. On his supervised sojourns outside to the deck, mole hunting became great sport.

My summer of butterflies included daily outings to discover the ever-changing patterns in my garden. With nose stuck deep within the impatiens, Yogurt's vigilance assured that butterflies and moles alike kept their distance. However, the busyness of our lives blinded me, initially, as to how ill Yogurt was really becoming.

Rather than terminate his life, at the end of July I elected for surgery to remove a large intestinal growth. Then came the butterflies of hope. I can still see my little guy running down the veterinary's hallway on the day I picked him up after his surgery, complaining loudly as if to say, "Let's blow this joint!" That we did, on one of those oppressively still and hazy summer evenings. Curiously enough, after his surgery we were both at peace.

Once again, I turned the porch light out, content to see him curled tightly around his incisions and blanketed by summer evening sounds. Yogurt was back home. Somehow things just felt more complete.

Mr. Yogurt rallied after his surgery, basically assisted by morning and evening prednisone to combat his cancerous malignancy. In fact, August and September saw him with boundless energy, almost as if he had returned to kittenhood. However, he was failing swiftly when the time came for his October veterinary visit, and a second lump was then identified. Since his appetite was nonexistent, his energies were saved for daily trips outside. After all, the moles and butterflies still had to be investigated.

The decision to terminate Yogurt's life was one of the most agonizing of my life. When I called to make the dreaded appointment, the telephone receiver felt as if it were a weighted barbell that just couldn't be lifted. The onset of November had brought some unseasonably mild weather, and Yogurt was still mustering his energy to go outside.

The misty evening before our veterinary appointment, Yogurt and I struggled to the back deck. The two of us sat under the porch light for a very long time. We had shared almost a decade of life together. That was soon to come to an end.

Yogurt had over an hour outdoors in the morning. His body was still and without energy. Then it was finally time for us to go. It was one of those beautiful autumn days when sunlight plays through brilliant foliage colors. Just as I did when he was a kitten, I wrapped him in a bath towel and held him tightly to my chest for the whole trip. Tears flowed down my checks and onto Yogurt, making his pink ears wet. We both could see our saddened reflections in the windshield.

He hissed. I just cried.

We were the first morning appointment, and the veterinarian came out to sit with us in the reception area. We talked quietly about his illness, and then she asked if I was ready.

Ready? After all this time, how could I ever be ready to give him up? My heart felt large and stuck, pounding uncontrollably at the base of my throat. "Have you said your good-byes?" the vet asked. All the talks to myself about how I could stoically see this ordeal through vanished in the instant he was taken from my arms and carried down the hall. He was meowing plaintively.

Yogurt was euthanized.

Arriving back home, I found much-needed quiet on the screen porch. Comfort had come in the veterinary's words about energy merely shifting and never really dissipating.

There was still some of the warm November morning remaining. Looking down on my garden, my numbness was disturbed by a sudden downdraft—it was as if the winds were pushing subtle whispers to me through the leaves. *Yogurt was okay. Yogurt was okay.* There, alit on my impatiens, was now an array of yellow maple leaves. As I stared, they rippled just like my butterflies of summer and then fluttered about before the wind currents carried them off again.

Now, in my quiet moments, I have only to close my eyes and imagine the summer of my garden and butterflies. They are an ever-so-subtle reminder of the beauty and generosity of all that I have been given. Most importantly, they bring me close to feeling Yogurt's continued devotion and spirit. I will always see him among the butterflies of any summer.

Always.

Bud Man

1. Shoo! Shoo Away!

With the parched dog days of our El Niño-driven summer droning endlessly forward, the modicum of sanity I had remaining was challenged—a kind of sultry monotony settled in with the sweltering heat. It seemed to cling tightly and smother decency in human character. Curiously, a special gift came to me from this tediousness.

The gift of my learning to be more patient was in the form of a ragamuffin of a creature I subsequently named Bud Man. Early summer is when I first noticed the scrawny, brown tabby skulking in the back alleys surrounding 41 Breakstone Drive. For sure, it was no one's cat, just like the millions of other strays reported so matter-of-factly as sad statistical profiles. Bud Man was somebody else's problem. It always works that way.

In retrospect, I realized Bud Man had probably been dumped in this mixed commercial and residential area as a November kitten. Somehow he had managed to tough out the cold, rainy winter and spring.

With three household felines already in my charge, what I selfishly didn't want was yet another animal to worry about. What I also didn't need were the diseases he could transmit. Or, worse yet, having rabies lurking at my back doorstep!

I simply didn't want to see Bud Man. So, like everyone else, I ignored him. In fact, I remember initially shooing him away from 41 Breakstone Drive and watching his thin form scuttle past the garbage cans. He would dive for shelter between the broken masonry of the olive-shingled, dilapidated garage, which huddled beside the back alley driveway.

2. A Change of Heart

Bud Man began to gradually nag at my conscience. I hated having to deal with this during hot summer days crammed with busy schedules. However, in the end, I have to say that it was his melancholy cries that wrenched my heart. Quite simply, I could no longer stand by and do nothing.

Bud Man became *my* problem.

Bud's rounds usually brought him to 41 Breakstone Drive around 6:00 AM. Like clockwork, he perched on the back picnic table, awaiting his can of food served on a paper plate. Other than this early morning encounter, I really never saw him for the remainder of the day. He would eat voraciously, with the occasional blood-filled tick dropping onto the plate from his scabbed fur.

As the summer heat intensified, Bud Man's appetite dramatically waned. I knew that something had to be done quickly. Calling the municipal animal control officer would have been the simplest way out, but I just couldn't dispose of Bud Man that impersonally.

The alternatives for Bud Man were indeed bleak. I procrastinated.

When I did muster the courage to make a veterinary appointment intended to put Bud Man permanently out of his misery, he couldn't be found anywhere. The appointment had to be canceled.

What a scamp!

Now I had to deal with re-psyching myself for going through this ordeal again. It certainly would have been much more comfortable to just stop caring. But I couldn't do that either.

What to do? What to do?

3. The Capture

Sam, my dearest other half, was very vocal in his objections to my feeding Bud Man. But I cautiously continued, ever mindful that this creature could unexpectedly bite me during our feeding sessions. About three weeks after the first failed appointment, my conscience got the better of me and I made a second appointment. I had deliberately set the alarm ahead of Bud Man's early morning feeding time.

Then I quietly kept watch.

Completely oblivious to his impending fate, Bud Man predictably strolled down the alley around 6:00 AM. This time I was prepared with a cage, whose wire gates sat gaping just inside the tool shed door. Two scoops of food lured him in, and I snapped the shed door shut directly behind him. He was caught! Oh, did the complaining meows ever emanate from that shed!

Never having handled the creature, I was prepared for the worst in taking Bud Man to his appointment with destiny. There I was on an insufferably muggy morning, dressed in high-winter boots, thick gloves, and a goose-down coat. Armed like some gladiator as a precaution against getting bitten, I gingerly opened the shed door prepared to do battle. Beads of sweat suddenly condensed at the nape of my neck. Curse this unbearable humidity! The shed had fallen silent.

What I discovered was Bud Man curled up and asleep in the cage! His food plate had been licked clean. He hardly stirred as I gently shut the cage door. As he had led a life of constantly being on the run in the hostile outdoors, I surmised this was the first time Bud Man had slept in peace, blanketed with a sense of security by the cage which now enveloped him.

4. Keeping the Appointment

His gentlemanly behavior certainly made the drive to the veterinary clinic more heart wrenching. I also instinctively knew I would be returning home without Bud Man.

"And who do we have here for today's appointment?"

"He doesn't have a name," I responded.

"Our records have to list *something*!" the office assistant chirped back. The tone of her voice annoyed me.

"Hum ... Buddy? No, let's call him Bud Man," was my rather firm retort.

On that fateful day, the first record of Bud Man's existence on the face of this planet was formally annotated. The poignancy of that moment made my throat feel lumpy and dry. In those minutes, I also recognized that I had become emotionally involved with the cat. With the cage door now gingerly swung open, the staff was fully prepared for restraining a berserk stray. The atmosphere in the small examination room was one of full alert.

Then Bud Man emerged.

Ironically, he entered with an air of almost regal calmness. Everybody in that tiny room simultaneously exhaled. Bud Man, who remained quite subdued during the ensuing medical poking, prodding, and pill popping, exhibited boundless curiosity about his new surroundings. He absolutely loved all the attention!

5. Time for a Decision

The veterinarian and I discussed Bud Man's options in the five agonizing minutes of awaiting test results for the highly transmittable and deadly feline leukemia. With his capture, I thought I was doing what was best for him. At least that's what my inner voice kept in dialogue with me about.

Bud Man tested positive. Up to this point, I was mostly in control of my emotions. My thoughts turned briefly to how I had come to anticipate his early AM feedings. The sounds of summer daybreak had given a kind of peace to both our souls.

"The only option is putting him to sleep, isn't it?" The words were extremely difficult for me.

Suddenly the room was immersed in an awkward silence, except for Bud Man gingerly wending his way through the countertop collection of medical supplies. Oblivious to all, he finally perched on the weight scale, content and purring. He trusted us implicitly with his fate.

6. The Decision

The veterinarian excused herself from the room, and for the next ten agonizing minutes it was just Bud Man and me.

Will this ever be over?

When the exam door reopened, a paper was thrust in front of my face. I signed Bud Man over to the clinic. The decision to take Bud Man's life was now out of my hands. I abruptly left the examination room, but not before seeing this trusting, gentle creature being hauled under an aide's arm to the back room and out of sight.

"As part of signing this agreement, you must never ask what happened to Bud Man," the veterinarian emphatically stated. Her words were bitter medicine for my heart. She went on to reiterate that finding a suitable home would be difficult, at best, because of the feline leukemia situation. To emphasize her point, she carefully repeated the part of her admonition about never asking after Bud Man's fate.

I clearly understood.

7. A Touch of the Bittersweet

Paying the office visit bill and then quickly departing, I just couldn't wait to reach the comfort of Breakstone Drive. However, the return trip was woefully empty. For the remainder of that hot summer, I frequently caught myself carrying a cup of coffee outside in the early morning hours and listening for Bud Man in the interminable heat. I came to realize that he had become a part of all that surrounded me.

What had I done?

I harbored deep regrets about the course of my actions. It was my doing that had taken his life away. If there were ever a next time, I simply would not get involved. No, not ever again.

Bud Man's story would have been over had it not been for our favorite red tabby's annual examination.

Sushi's routine September appointment for updating his shots included the usual back-and-forth banter between the veterinarian and myself. Painstakingly avoiding the topic of Bud Man, I really felt more comfortable in not knowing his fate but always thinking that there had been a positive outcome. Of course, I kept wondering.

Interestingly, it was the veterinarian herself who casually surfaced the topic. I was stunned.

"Do you remember Bud Man?" she asked.

Did she think I could forget him so easily? I stiffened and leaned into her next words.

"Believe me—you don't have to worry about him!" She was now smiling. "Trust me, he's well taken care of and in a good home. Incidentally, he's turned out to be quite a character."

I just simply couldn't believe what I was hearing. Bud Man was alive! My immediate reaction was to hug the vet out of shear joy. Whether it was appropriate etiquette or not to hug one's veterinarian is a question that shall remain unanswered. I did it anyway.

The Bud Man news was so upbeat that I failed to notice Sushi's disappearance until late that same day. After a search, I found him cowering under our guest bed with a severe allergic reaction to his booster shots. He was burning to the touch and drooling from such a high fever. His eyes were tightly closed. Thoughts of Bud Man dissolved into focusing completely on Sushi's alarming condition.

The next couple weeks of intravenous feedings brought Sushi back to us. I couldn't help but think that eight of his nine lives were gone, and it's this ninth one that our household had left to enjoy.

8. A Matter of Trust and Faith

Perhaps it is mostly through the experience of everyday living that personal character is indelibly and uniquely traced. We become, in essence, an intricacy of fine lines etched on our very soul, as if it were leaded crystal. Our major traumas make deeper grooves, but it is the daily stuff that really inscribes the very design of our individuality.

Summer's sultriness intruded deep into October before resigning to crisper weather. What a welcome relief! As I traipsed through autumn's fallen, colorful leaves, I couldn't help but be in a more reflective mood. In a curious way, the whole episode with Bud Man had become a touchstone. It was a lesson in care giving for me. It was about offering undivided love and then having to painfully let go and simply trust all would turn out for the best. In its purest essence, I suspect, that is what faith is really all about.

9. A Final Twist and Turn

The letter and photograph of Bud Man arrived about six months later. I was dumbfounded! Here was this handsome animal posing in a slightly opened drawer of what looked like an antique, French-styled writing desk. Bud Man had certainly found the right home. The curious twist was that it turned out to be the veterinarian's personal residence!

Then came a very poignant turn. About the time of our Bud Man letter, Sam and I were faced with having to give up Sushi after a lingering and painful dying process. Opting for the euthanasia alternative one warm February morning was another one of those gut-wrenching decisions.

Ironically, Sushi's fate had once more become inextricably interwoven with news of Bud Man.

Chapter 6: Fire Bugs in the Night Desert

A final mélange

Firebugs in the Night Desert

Subconsciously
we slather
ourselves
in opacity,
painstakingly
preoccupied
with guarding
against
dangerous inner shadows
remorseful thoughts
and how
we perceive
others
may think and feel
about us.

Thank goodness
for
firebugs
in the
night desert.

Spontaneously
glimmering
distilling
illuminating
joyful, poetic
unexpected rhythms
of life
they entice
and
mesmerize
us into
careless abandonment
of our inner selves.

At such moments
there is
simply
nothing more to do
than dance
wonderfully
in their light.

Night Flight

Cities lie below
As glassed orbs
Plummeted into the
Black earth-abyss.

Kinetic blue-white splinters
Shattering into morning.

Day Flight

Tree shadows lie below like
Payne's Gray dabbled
On white snow.

Huddling, cragged forms
Now stiffening into
Contours of the frozen
River's edge.

The Christmas Ornament Collection

I. The Red Gingham Birds

Without a lingering thought, our Christmas ornaments are hurriedly repacked into boxes for storage after the New Year's celebrations. Standing sentinel over the season's bric-a-brac and then shoved to the farthermost dusty corners of the attic, they are soon forgotten.

"Babes, where *did* we put those boxes of Christmas ornaments from last year?"

With the new holiday season approaching, the frantic searching begins. Somewhere among the entanglement of Christmas lights and life-size, vine-woven reindeer shrouded in plastic dry cleaning bags, the cache of ornaments is rediscovered.

Our Christmas ornament collection is meant to be savored. This is one of those special moments sandwiched between impulsiveness to get the tree all decorated and quiet reflection. As each ornament is gingerly unwrapped from its protective, crumpled tissue paper, reminiscences ignite the imagination like fireflies.

There are the handmade ornaments as well as the store-bought ones. There are those we remember from childhood; those given in love and friendship, and those acquired as mementos of faraway places. All, indeed, are treasured!

The last to be opened is a nondescript box containing red gingham birds. It's a collection of a hundred or so, with each cotton fabric bird able to nest easily in the palm of your hand. They were a gift from my mother with her seamstress talents. She so adored Christmas, and, even in her eighties and with failing eyesight, she managed to craft these wonderful birds over a span of two years. They are certainly not among what would be considered our expensive ornaments. But, in their homey, small, uneven hand stitching are woven priceless hours of love and joy.

Every year, our finishing touch is to place this flock of red gingham birds on the lowest branches of our Christmas tree. It truly is a magical moment as we stand back and admire our handiwork. Those little gingham birds appear to lift the tree in flight. In so doing, they fill our home with the glorious spirit of the holiday season.

2. Globes of Colored Glass

Thank goodness for F. W. Woolworth & Co.'s popularization, at the turn of the century, of glass Christmas balls. These wonderfully simple colored glass ornaments always seem to find their rightful niche among more ostentatious Christmas ornamentation. Nowadays, they're all gussied up in frosted designer colors, but it's really the old-fashioned ones I'm thinking of. It's wonderful in a quiet moment to discover the complexity of reflections in their shiny surfaces. The world these little glass globes adorn is precisely mirrored back through brilliant hues of red, gold, blue, and green. An inquisitive glance is rewarded with fascinating images of tree lights, sunlight piercing through windowpanes, and even self-portraits!

Last year our holiday season was ushered in via close friends' written invitation to tour seasonally bedecked homes. Our friend's husband had had some health problems, but it was certainly nothing to keep us from touring. Just as children unwrapping gifts on Christmas morning, we ogled resplendent Christmas decorations as each front door on the tour cracked open. Oh, the scents of vanilla, evergreen, and spices were deliciously intermingled! And, of course, down to the very last decorated tree, there were the unobtrusive globes of colored glass. In our wonderment of four faces perfectly reflected back to us in a single, tiny orb, we just had to smile. We had such a good time.

About a week before Christmas, when all the holiday decoration boxes resurfaced, our entrance hall looked like a field after a paper war. Our earlier tour of homes had most certainly inspired us to new decorating heights.

That is when the unexpected phone call came.

Overnight, our friend's husband had been admitted to the local hospital's intensive care unit. We were advised that congestive heart failure was imminent. The stacked boxes of Christmas decorations stood in our hallway like inert solders on this Christmas Eve. Everything waited.

We were already in the car when a thought stuck me. "Wait, I've got to run back inside. It will only take a moment!" Frantically rummaging through the boxes of decorations, I found what I was searching for and gently tucked it in a pocket of my oversized winter coat. Off to the hospital we drove.

He beamed when I pulled from my pocket the little glass Christmas ornament, the azure of a Caribbean sea. The grogginess caused by continuous intravenous feeding tubes and doses of morphine couldn't arrest his hidden delight. In the glass globe, once again, were collected together the reflections of all our faces. On this Christmas Eve, they were countenances of hope in just making it through the night.

I will always remember the poignancy of that Christmas Eve. It would be his final one. We will forever miss him, and I know that somewhere among the holiday season's globes of colored glass, his presence reassuringly lingers and smiles on us.

Chapter 7: Lessons from the Zoological Park

The mesquite bosque and its life lessons

Preface

Life in the desert is not for everyone.

Desert living is about extremes. Extremes are in the weather: pre-monsoon summertime temperatures soar to a daily 100 degrees or higher, and dry, silent desert winter nights plummet to bone-freezing temperatures, bearing witness to snow-encrusted cacti.

Extremes are reflected in the people who seek the desert lifestyle. The desert is a magnet for individuals thirsting for radical change in their lives—a purging or rebirth of sorts. The desert is a place of camouflage to stealthily move through and not be recognized. Some come to the desert to heal. Some venture to the desert to meet its challenges of living and surviving head on. Some come to the desert to bide their time and then die.

However, it is the extremes of the desert that impart a genuine sense of freedom and artistic expression. Much of the desert landscape is painted in muted shades of gray-brown, most of it sand, dirt, and rock. The desert vegetation provides a small interlude of green, but it is certainly not comforting like grand deciduous or conifer-treed forests and flowered meadowlands. Yet, a gut-wrenching excitement of life is here. It's in the earth-jolting strikes of monsoon lightening against the roiling, purple sky. It's in the ephemeral beauty of the night-blooming cereus cactus. It's in observing the swift, silent, and deadly dances of hunter and hunted.

To simply move into a house and live under the desert sky is one thing. It is a much larger challenge to make a welcoming home—to create and surround oneself with a place of shelter from the elements, a place of beauty that will stimulate the senses, and an environment of vegetative richness. One could say that it's almost going against the nature of the unforgiving desert, and, in some ways, it certainly is!

The following are vignettes about the desert's real richness and abundance of life. Build a place of respite from the searing summer sun and freezing winter nights, and the desert will come to you, offering life lessons if you are open and listen for them.

Our desert property also has a casita, and over the years we have hosted a number of guests from across the world. These fascinating people journeying to the desert have certainly enriched our lives as we sit together and share stories over an evening cocktail. However, their tales are reserved for another time and place. To some degree or another, they too have come to the desert to experience its energy.

Greater Roadrunner

A solitary greater roadrunner occasionally passed through our desert property, or so we thought. They were never a problem, but then there wasn't much on our land to interest them. More importantly, we weren't there to pay attention to what was happening.

This spring we started to change the surroundings of the wash area winding through our property. The desert wash is bone-dry all year, except for when the outburst of seasonal monsoon rains gush off the mountain boulders and careen across our acreage. Our thinking was that this spot of desert and wash area could become a fabulous wildlife center of sorts. We would provide some water and build a shaded structure for growing herbs. We would also throw out some seeds and, over our morning coffee, leisurely watch the small birds feed.

The unintended consequence of our creating a ubiquitous watering hole and supplying seeds for the smaller birds is that the predatory roadrunner now boldly makes habitual stops in the light of day. They are fearless and seldom back down when cornered. Their stops are not merely to quench thirst but an opportunity to hunt *anything* small that moves. The capture, pinching, and noisy death squawking of small birds being gulped down alive is a terribly hard act to witness for the novice desert nature watcher. The roadrunner's cunning and swiftness live up to its Walt Disney image, but the reality is certainly not a benign or comic image in any way.

The thought occurred to us that we could actually fix this situation, effectively restoring peace and quiet to our personal sanctuary. Our ingenious plan was to attempt to capture and relocate, within the vast desert, what we thought was *the* culprit—an individual roadrunner. Now that solitary roadrunner has turned into several of them, all seeking water and prey. Attempting to relocate what the natural rhythm of the desert brings to our doorstep is just plain silly on our part. Downright foolishness would probably be a more accurate word for our simple-minded plan!

The Greater Roadrunner has brought us the lesson that daytime predators are as lethal as those of the blackened night. You can't wish them away. They will forever stalk their prey among us, and in the end it is only our most deep-seeded instincts that keep us alive. These instincts and the luck of the draw in timing ourselves to avoid being prey at the watering holes of life certainly go hand in hand.

Ephemeral Beauty

Witnessing the desert's ephemeral beauty is a matter of timing. There is not just a single point of time in which stunning beauty appears. Rather, points of vibrancy emerge throughout the desert seasons.

This desert beauty is no more evident than in the cactus family. Most of us never give these curious plants a second thought, and, if encountered, the humble cactus is generally confined to a small coffee table-sized planter in a sunny corner of Grandma's house, usually gathering dust. After all, they're pesky, prickly specimens—definitely not to be touched. That, of course, begs the question of why one would have such plants around.

In the aridness of the desert, one encounters more cacti specimens, shapes, and sizes than ever imagined! Either you are fascinated or repulsed by them. There seems to be no middle ground, as with many things that are integral to desert living. The fact that the Southwest has entire nurseries and greenhouses dedicated to propagating these curiosities is mystifying to desert newcomers.

Of course, the first sightings and close-up encounters with the towering saguaro cacti—the giant sentinels of the desert landscape—generally leave even the most cacti-adverse among us in awe. After all, the saguaros, particularly those with the drama of appendages reaching skyward against purple and orange sunsets, have lived more than twice the length of our lifetimes. These are not merely plants. The saguaros seem to be timeless entities, silently bearing witness across the decades.

The bloom of a flower is classic ephemeral beauty—all flowers and all blooms. We take these blooms for granted—the wildflowers we whiz by along the highway, the dozen perfect rose blooms given most thoughtfully by a treasured heart, and the ocean-side summer gardens with riots of flower blossoms crowding along white picket fences, nodding in the sea breezes. We are fairly nonchalant about the flowers that surround us. They will always be there and available to us. Those blooms are etched in our memories.

However, in the harshness of the desert environment, with summer's blistering sunrays and winter's bone-cold frosts, comes the unexpected gift of a cactus bloom. The annual wait for these visually stunning beauties is always worth it as the flowers pop up between thorny spines and knotted joints. A day or so is perhaps their total, fleeting lifespan. Yet, their moment in the desert sunshine reflects absolutely stunning and delicate ephemeral beauty. It is sometimes difficult to imagine such beauty coming from this most unlikely source.

Examining these cactus blooms makes me wonder how many other nondescript things we pass every day that carry ephemeral beauty—we just don't see it in *its* moment. Perhaps we should move through our adult worlds with at least a modicum of consciousness and childlike awareness. The magnificent cacti blooms have taught me to seek beauty in unexpected places.

Schnickel Puss

"Schnickel Puss" was a term of endearment my German-born father used to call me. I was his second daughter. As I grew up and he passed, the term faded into my very-distant memory. That was, at least, until the grand move to desert living!

It took about three seasons for the round-tailed ground squirrels to discover our property. Maybe we had such fertile digging ground because the rock-hardened layer of desert caliche was buried at least a couple feet below the surface. We were fortunate, since those with caliche close to the surface literally have to use a jackhammer to make a hole large enough to plant anything—even the common geranium or pansy. That's why pots are really popular in desert landscaping!

Well, last season a colony of ground squirrels seemed to move in, and entrances to burrows began popping up all over. For desert-dwelling animals, holes are something pretty special, used both for waiting out the intense heat of summer afternoons and escaping from most predators. Rather than taking the common gardener's stance that the only good ground squirrel is a deceased one, we did little to prevent these fellows from their colonization of our property. Our adoption of the live-and-let-live philosophy was soon to be challenged.

With a cup of morning joe in hand, I found it amusing to watch what was happening in our fenced-in mesquite tree bosque. By midsummer, each of our weathered mesquites had a mound of dug-up dirt at its base and a resident ground squirrel standing watch. The grove was a bustling place, indeed. From somewhere in the deep recesses of my brain came the name, "Schnickel Puss," for the resident ground squirrel closest to our lookout post. For most of the summer we watched Schnickel Puss live out his days fairly adeptly, dodging predators mostly in the form of red-tailed hawks and golden eagles. It was part of my morning coffee ritual to check on the Schnickel Puss mound and leave an offering of a peanut or two.

That same summer we awoke one day to the gut-wrenching decision that euthanasia was the best recourse for our failing, elderly tabby cat. Consequently, it was as if time stood still and the rhythms of our home and property came to a screeching halt. Everything was out of balance after we put our pet to sleep. I could just feel it all around me. The first incident the week after we lost our last kitty in a line of several cats, occurred when a mourning dove severely mangled its leg on one of our wrought-iron bird feeders and dangled upside down by its mostly severed leg until early morning, when it could be freed. Unfortunately, the second incident involved Schnickel Puss.

Daily chores required crisscrossing the mesquite bosque landscape. What caught the corner of my eye was a head slowly bobbing up and down from inside the Schnickel Puss hole. How strange! The ground squirrels usually plunged completely out of sight at the sound or vibration of human footsteps. Now one was playing peek-a-boo with me? This just had to be checked out.

Getting down on my hands and knees for a better look, I completely froze. I was not staring at Schnickel Puss, but rather a cream color snake head! And this was a very large snake head, at that, with dark stripes from in front of its eyes and angling to its jaw! In the dark of night, the reptile must have slithered onto our property through the desert wash area in his quest for prey. I immediately sensed the ground squirrel's fate. The serpent I now faced in the squirrel's hole had most certainly gulped down Schnickel Puss. Instinctively I knew this would be a battle of wits, as I am terrified of snakes—any kind of snake. And this guy was likely to be of a venomous variety. However, I made up my mind that Schnickel Puss simply had to be avenged.

"Oh, that's just a gopher snake," was the observation casually offered by the pool maintenance person who had just emerged on the chaotic scene. "They're not poisonous." Well, what a relief that was! Nevertheless, the problem still remained. The enemy had to go, one way or another. The laissez-faire theory of desert living and providing sanctuary to *all* who come just flew out the window. Fate had to be altered at this point.

For my husband and me, it was a battle of wits to wrangle that snake, but we did it! Desert etiquette dictates that such creatures be captured and released back into more remote desert. Ours was not a kill operation. Were we shocked when we swung our trusty frog-gigging pole and lassoed the head of the gopher snake to extract him from the squirrel hole? Yes, indeed! This snake was enormous, extending over six feet in length, and its hefty girth certainly included an ample supply of ground squirrels. Our pole, with the huge snake dangling from the other end, was not a tidy sight. Unlike the medical Wand of Hermes with perfectly entwined snakes forming a double helix, our catch was a scaly, knotted, continuously moving ball of rust color blotches.

I knew that Schnickel Puss was a goner. Now we just had to do the snake-release thing in a remote desert wash. And that became another story in itself.

When we returned home after releasing this abominable creature, all we could do was stare at the scene of the ground squirrel tragedy. In an odd way, it seemed an appropriate and quite soothing thing to do. I could not even imagine the horror of having the breath of life slowly squeezed out by such a monster. A real sense of sadness filled the remaining morning hours until we saw *it*. Could we believe what we were seeing? There was Schnickel Puss, cautiously returning to his hole, but only skirting its perimeter. The scent of snake-as-enemy must have saturated the ground squirrel's sanctuary. It was no longer safe here. The last time we saw Schnickel Puss, he was high-tailing it for a fence gate which led into a new patch of desert reserved for utility right-of-ways. He was searching for his new home.

In fact, the remaining ground squirrels populating our mesquite bosque also disappeared, and that part of out desert landscape turned silent and still. Encouraged by the Santa

Ana winds, time smoothed over all the ground squirrel mounds. Mesquite bean and leaf debris clogged the holes. It was as if all the ground squirrel mounds had been buried in the sands of time like the pyramids of some ancient civilization. Summer blended into fall, and then the chilling, opaque nights of the winter desert set in.

The desert begins to wake again in the warming sun and the kiss of brief rains in late January. Frosts remain a danger at night, but the days are simply glorious. It was on one of these days that I happened to glance out towards the gnarled mesquite tree that had once provided shelter for Schnickel Puss. There sat a ground squirrel, and the old hole was now open! I had to believe that this newcomer was the legacy of Schnickel Puss, perhaps even an immediate offspring.

I now feel that equilibrium is returning to our little piece of the desert. Maybe our upcoming summer can again be spent, in part, watching ground squirrels colonize our mesquite tree grove. I surmise that it was me who didn't have faith in the cycles of nature and the incredible instincts we are all given to survive.

The other lesson for me was that when you open yourself to accepting what comes— whether it is ideas, people, or nature—you have to be prepared for the consequences. What arrives in your world is not always what you are prepared to deal with. But then you are suddenly forced to.

The Nightwalkers

Our property is fenced, and yet they come.

The nocturnal desert, including the night sky above, is a restless place. It is a landscape of constant movement. Human desert dwellers fence in their property to keep the wildness of the desert at arm's length. There is good reason for this, which you understand when you are suddenly awakened by the eerie surrounding night sounds. The coyote pack yelping as it encircles its cornered prey sends goose bumps up a sleeper's arms. Observing the massive wingspan of the great horned owl as it cruises low and so close against the moonlit sky is witnessing the age-old hunter's dance. A snorting pack of javelina consuming anything remotely edible against your back door is disconcerting in the middle of the night.

Then there are those that travel in silence. The coati, raccoons, and an occasional bobcat reveal their presence on our property through footprints stamped into the sands of our wash area. Initially, it was quite startling to discover both the size and variety of paw prints left by our nightly hunters. Now we take such discoveries in stride. The nightwalkers are not discriminating about their prey, and beloved domestic animals, such as cats and dogs, can become easy prey if they are exposed to the unforgiving desert night. The night is about life and death. The night is about just surviving.

I suppose it was arriving home on a late fall night when our car headlights crossed a set of gleaming eyes in our rock garden, which adjoins the road. This part of our property is not fenced, so I'm sure that it was prime hunting grounds for what turned out to be a black feral cat. As best as we could determine, this cat's home was across the way and down another wash, with its sandy edges crowded with thorny ocotillo and six-foot tall, pancake-thin prickly pear cacti. Maybe the cat's misfortune in life began with the stigma of being born as a black kitten. Anyway, this guy was one of those millions of strays that are dumped at the edge of town and somehow survive. We would see him occasionally, always on the other side of the road. I nicknamed him "Panther."

It was a rainy, winter desert day when I glanced through my Spanish-style, arched office window. The Santa Catalina Mountains were presenting themselves in the richness of their deep, wet earth tones, and the water brimming over the wash across the street appeared to flow directly from the mountain foothills. Movement in our street-side rock garden extracted me from my quiet reverie. I just had never seen one *this* size! The coyote crouching within fifty yards of my window was huge and sleek. The rain certainly did not faze this denizen of the desert. It was almost as if the coyote was posing and preening in the daylight, wanting attention. All the alarms went off in my head as I realized the coyote had sauntered from the exact same wash that served as Panther's home. If Panther were still alive, in any encounter this coyote would most certainly rip the cat to shreds.

Later that day as I made my rounds between our mesquite bosque and wash areas, I spotted Panther crouched among our woodpiles. He had somehow snuck through the wash and onto our fenced property, seeking refuge and safety from the coyote. As we knew our new resident was an adept hunter, discovering him on our property was met with mixed emotions. Piles of dove feathers and the vestiges of wings were daily findings. The answer, I thought, was to place a bowl of dried cat food on the workbench in the tool shed. The idea that cat food had to be much tastier than fresh-killed dove meat was foolish thinking on my part. Panther became our resident feral, and the bird killings continued into the chilling December days of the winter desert. What I hadn't realized was that an innocuous bowl of cat food would turn into a magnet for other nightwalkers.

I was startled one early evening by the size of the raccoon that had his face in the cat food bowl. We frightened each other! The raccoon quickly waddled off between the lumber piles, and I charged off in the opposite direction for the safety of the house. As the days progressed, Panther became a nightly visitor to the food bowl, and I could not help but wonder how he was coping as the desert night temperatures dropped well below freezing. There was nothing else I could do for him—there was no shelter he would trust. He was too far gone and much too wild to ever trust a human being. It really was sad.

One early morning replenishment of the food bowl brought me face to face with yet another night visitor in the form of a skittish, half-grown, gray tabby kitten. I didn't need more cat troubles, so with an agitated, "Shoo away!" I chased the new arrival back through the wash and off our property. It undoubtedly belonged to a neighbor and was no longer my problem. However, this kitten problem *did* return.

The Sonoran Desert mid-December days were a balmy sixty degrees, but the nights were turning a penetrating cold. Panther continued to pounce on birds within the bounds of our property, and the tabby kitten with its sad green eyes continued to visit our shed and food bowl. About the time I decided that something had to be done, the kitten abruptly changed its behavior, running to greet us as we went on our daily chores through the mesquite bosque, coming close, but not close enough, to touch. In the week before Christmas, desert night temperatures were plummeting—it was time to capture the tabby. Armed with fireplace gloves and a heavy jacket to ward off the anticipated biting and scratching I was sure would follow, I strode out to our bosque one late afternoon and began coaxing the kitten. She did not come. I called. I waited. There was nothing to hear. Was she gone?

It was with a heavy heart that I started back to the house. The warmth of the sun was now totally disappearing, pushed away by the frosty night air rolling in over the wash. At the very moment the gate was closing, the stray tabby brushed closed to me. I looked down and snatched the kitten up, expecting the very worst of feral behavior. What I got instead was purring as we quickly headed towards the garage and her first night of food and shelter away from the nightwalkers in quite some time.

Obake (Japanese for "ghost") came to us seven months after our heartbreaking ordeal of loosing the last of a line of cherished but elderly feline companions. We did not choose this newest spirit of the house. Obi chose us and has gifted our house with boundless youthful energy. Coincidentally, she has identical color and markings and a similar disposition as our last cat. I would like to imagine that a Michelangelo-like hand of God emerged from the sky one moonlit desert night and carefully placed Obi in our care. However, the reality of Obake coming to us is probably closer to a car door silently opening in the middle of the night, a heartless hand rolling the small kitten out as fodder for the desert nightwalkers, and then the car driving off. Some would say that Obake's arrival is all just coincidence, but I'm not so sure anymore. In a curious way, the untamed Panther had been Obake's escort. In the days following, Panther disappeared permanently from our property. We surmised that he succumbed to a nightwalker more powerful than him. As for Obake, she has never once asked to venture back outside.

It wasn't simply caffeine that jolted me awake before I got to the gate of our mesquite bosque on a morning not too long after we took Obake in. Two dogs were bounding against the iron bars of the gate, barking and looking somewhat cranky and definitely hungry. How they got into our fenced property was anybody's guess. We were about to experience another set of nightwalkers.

One thing to know about stray dogs is that they should be approached *very* cautiously. And that I did! With my husband's words of encouragement being broadcast from a safe distance, I held my breath and gently pushed open the gate. Oh, my! Here was a small cocker spaniel and his companion, a gangly, black-haired dog, yelping and jumping all over me. They were a shivering, hungry twosome who had obviously spent the night in our mesquite bosque. Thank goodness the cocker spaniel had a readable dog tag with a phone number.

Disappointingly, no one was home at the number. "Yes, we found Archimedes and friend," was the excited voice mail we left, along with our address and phone number. We then waited for a return call to solve this newest puzzle. It seemed these companions had escaped their fenced compound and wandered through the night desert for several miles. In fact, Archimedes was limping by the time we discovered him, having fallen victim to thorny desert brambles. In the night, a passing car had encountered the two panicked dogs wandering along a roadside, and the driver's only thought was to dump them over a nearby fence to save them from predatory nightwalkers. That fence happened to be our mesquite bosque, and that mesquite bosque happened to be their sanctuary for making it through the night. And that they did! Our canine visitors, the black dog being named Socrates, were soon returned to their rightful owners, and our mesquite bosque resumed its usual, quieter rhythm.

We continue to host an array of desert nightwalkers, but none are quite so memorable as Panther, Obake, Archimedes, and Socrates. The desert nightwalkers occasionally touch our human world with a whole other world of life and death drama. Like many things in life, there are times when a person can positively intervene, and there are other times when you are simply powerless. It is nature's way for only the strongest and cleverest of the nightwalkers to survive among us to walk yet another night.

The Feathered Kingdom

Plethora is probably too sophisticated a word, but it is certainly accurate in describing the variety of birds that migrate through our property. The desert is an amazing place, hosting everything from the tiniest species of iridescent hummingbirds to colonies of Gila woodpeckers busily carving their shelters and raising their broods in the "boots" of the mighty saguaro cacti. However, it is the ground feeding fowl that have offered me life lessons. These birds are not as agile or are just short-distance flyers by their very nature. This is certainly a huge disadvantage in the desert ecosystem, as the ground feeders frequently become the hunted.

The mourning dove is the universal symbol of peace and innocence. Yet, this bird is relentlessly stalked by desert birds of prey. The mourning dove attempts to blend into the desert rocks and sand with its gray-brown colorings and a look of innocence in its round, dark eyes. However, most of the time the dove cannot outwit its hunter, as the doves are sadly equipped with neither speed nor agility. It is a kind of quiet, noble death that the mourning dove submits to under razor-sharp talons. There is no squealing or squawking as these gentle creatures are literally pulled apart, with a fury of feathers flying gently back to the earth. I am now mellowing in my senior years and find myself asking the "why" question less and less. This is something that I personally have had to come to terms with. Those of innocence and peace are often hunted—even to death. It is simply the law of nature.

Our towering olive tree in the courtyard is a favorite night roosting spot for many ground feeders, including mourning doves and the desert-dwelling Gambel's Quail. Sunset imparts a sense of urgency in those seeking shelter, and it is really quite entertaining to witness the single-file parade of feathered creatures launching from our stone wall into the tree boughs. This magnificent olive tree surely had to be the safest of havens, guarding fragile life through the desert night. At least, that is what I thought until one night when a great horned owl made pass after sweeping pass into the silver-green olive tree, aggressively hunting our nesting birds. The scene was wild with the disturbed, chaotic flight of the hunter and the many birds being hunted. As I witnessed the owl's enormous wingspan fan against the full moon in silhouette, I could not help but think of

Native American symbolism. Connected with darkness and the night, the owl is believed to be the departed soul of a loved one. *Who had just visited us?* With a sudden chilling wind through the leaves, the great owl abruptly departed for other hunting grounds. He had not been successful here, this night. To the best of my awareness, neither the great horned owl, nor the spirits he carried, visited our property again. Every now and then I reflect on this commanding owl's dramatic visit as an omen in the midst of everyday life. Maybe omens are something only the spiritually gifted among us can read and understand. For me, this imposing nocturnal visitor left quite an impression, but it was a sign that I simply could not read. Once again, I was quite content when a sense of calmness returned to the property. Perhaps I'm preoccupied with the present and living in the mundane. Possibly I need to exercise more introspection as my sixties decade grows very close. The appearance of this magnificent great horned owl has definitely made me think about that.

With their forward-curling plume, Gambel's Quail are some of the most fascinating of desert ground feeders. They have the gift of flight, but only for short distances to avoid predators such as snakes, hawks, bobcats, and coyote. Being extremely gregarious, coveys of quail move together through the thorny desert vegetation, constantly seeking seeds and protection. Curiously, Gambel's Quail remain mostly monogamous. If a mate is lost, the survivor of the pair attempts to guard and raise the chicks alone. We spotted such a survivor feeding at the seed block on our property. There was indeed a nervous aura about this new father as he circled his only remaining offspring, and one could just imagine the tragedies he had witnessed in the rest of his quail family being annihilated one by one. So now, in this evening hour, there were just the two of them—father and chick—in the vast desert world. It was a touching sight to behold, and we watched them until dusk blended into night. It would have all been so comforting had it not been for the sudden arrival of a solitary Cooper's hawk above our feeding grounds. We all surveyed each other. We all froze in place, except for the chick, which bounded about with the energy of discovering his world that evening and was oblivious to the impending threat. The hawk's attack came swiftly amidst an explosion of birds seeking cover from the formidable predator. Fortunately, our quail chick was caught in brambles and instinctively assumed a motionless posture, but the chick's father had taken flight for his very life, and the hawk was in close pursuit of him. After the attack, a sullen quiet returned to our feeding grounds. It was now totally dark, and we knew that father and chick were very much separated—the chick was frantically running from underneath one creosote bush to another. Of course, in the morning there was no chick to be seen.

Sometimes it is just more comfortable to live with hope than to think about the grimmer alternatives. That is the lesson I have taken from these social desert quail. I prefer to think that the noble quail father and his tiny, solitary chick were reunited somewhere on the other side of our property fence line and are quietly going about their desert existence. You reach an age in life where you just cannot afford to mentally dwell on the negative. It takes all the energy you can muster to fend off chilling thoughts about aging and the termination of your life on earth. It is *hope* that keeps you going.

Some Final Thoughts

Our mesquite bosque is not always about the predator and its prey. The stand of stately, gnarled trees provides refuge for animals that are sick, injured, or very near death. They seem to be drawn to the energy of our property. Like all of life, the body's spirit eventually fades quietly away, without fanfare and without tears. The desert elements take over then, with feathers scattering like tumbleweeds across the dusty desert floor and small animal carcasses withering to nothing in the bleaching summer sun. We try to do what we can to provide that extra shelter, but we cannot stop the inevitable natural drama of life and death continuously being played out before our eyes.

I am certainly at the time in my life when I am most open to life lessons quite literally being carried out on my doorstep. A Gambel's Quail nest carefully tended to in one of my larger flower pots offers a microcosm of lessons. The fact that this nest continued to exist day after day, undisturbed and hidden away from the desert predators, was in itself somewhat of a miracle. However, the quiet warmth of a very early summer desert morning and the chaos of quail hatchlings belied the absolute struggle for survival going on in that flower pot. The mother quail left immediately after the hatching with only the strongest of her chicks and did not return. The weakest were left behind, chirping loudly into the evening hours and growing weaker without their mother's body heat. The quail chicks that were injured in falls from the pot died close to the nest. And then there were the seemingly infertile eggs, finally left in open view and an easy meal for predators. The cycle of birth, life, survival, reuse, death—it was all there, playing out in my pot! It was only by happenstance that I happened to witness everything, and, of course, the quail situation certainly played on my most primordial fears.

I grasp at the hope that I will be remembered on this earth in some small way when I die and my spirit wafts into some ethereal realm. My most deep-seated fear is being like these desert animals—slipping from earthly life mostly unnoticed and immediately forgotten. But in the continuum of eternal time, that's how it is for all of us. We are but a moment, and our personal footprint is minuscule. Just when I am in my most remorseful mental state, a pair of ravens unexpectedly soars overhead. According to legend, the enormous raven is a creature of change and the keeper of the secrets of the cosmos. How ironic that these two black ravens linger and lazily circle our mesquite bosque above where I am standing in my darkest reverie. I am left with the image of the raven's silhouette against the day's desert sunset, which now broadcasts crimson and orange hues through the tree branches. I am also left feeling very small but very much connected with the desert's circle of life.

There is a kind of peace I possess tonight as I depart the mesquite bosque and our zoological park. It is breathtaking when you think you have caught just a glimmer of some of the most basic truths in the natural universe—the truths that repeat themselves for eternity. The epiphany, to me, was how simple life really is and how complex and mysterious we choose to make it. The cycles of life will happen to us all. Each of us will have our day in the sun, and then we will quietly dissolve into time. The inevitability of it all makes growing older quite a revelation. In my last decades of earthly life, this is a much more tolerable and comfortable mental and emotional place to be. It is about being in a position of acceptance.

All of a sudden, purplish clouds and accompanying lightning become visible through our mountain pass. This change in weather captures my attention as I race to the back door. Our desert monsoon season has arrived with its downpours of life-giving rain. Rather than seeking shelter, I choose to stand where I am and enjoy the freedom of being soaked to the skin. It is my cleansing.